# Becoming a
# TEACHER

# Becoming a
# TEACHER

Jefferson Twp. Public Library
1031 Weldon Road
Oak Ridge, NJ 07438
(973) 208-6115

LEARNINGEXPRESS®

NEW YORK

Library of Congress Cataloging-in-Publication Data
Becoming a teacher.—1st ed.
    p.  cm.
  ISBN 978-1-57685-693-2
  1. Teaching—Vocational guidance.
  LB1775.B4127  2009
  371.10023'73—dc22          2009013863

Printed in the United States of America

9 8 7 6 5 4 3 2 1

First Edition

ISBN 978-1-57685-693-2

**Regarding the Information in This Book**
Every effort has been made to ensure the accuracy of directory information up until press
time. However, phone numbers and/or addresses are subject to change. Please contact the
respective organization for the most recent information.

For more information or to place an order, contact LearningExpress at:
  2 Rector Street
  26th Floor
  New York, NY 10006

Or visit us at:
  www.learnatest.com

# Contents

# Introduction:
# Are You Teaching Material?

*The mediocre teacher tells. The good teacher explains. The superior teacher demonstrates. The great teacher inspires.*

—William Arthur Ward

**TEACHING IS** a unique career in which you will wear many hats—communicator, disciplinarian, evaluator, classroom manager, counselor, decision maker, role model, and even surrogate parent.

According to 2009's *The MetLife Survey of the American Teacher: Past, Present, and Future*, a retrospective survey report, teacher satisfaction has increased over the last quarter century. Today's teachers feel more respected by society and more capable of earning a decent salary. The survey also found that far more teachers today—75% compared with 45% in 1984—would recommend a career in teaching.

Is teaching for you? What are your specialty and grade-level preferences? How do you choose a teacher education program, and more importantly, how do you pay for it? What can you expect from your teacher training? How about your first year on the job? This book explains all this and more.

Maybe you've envisioned yourself in front of a bustling classroom since you were a young student. You may have been inspired by an innovative teacher or a subject you were passionate about. Perhaps one of your parents was a teacher who entertained the family with classroom stories over dinner. Or maybe you're a community college or college student who has just started thinking about a teaching career and taking courses to prepare. Maybe you have been working for a while in another field and desire the career satisfaction experienced by the teachers you know. Whatever your situation, if you think you *might* want to be a teacher—or if you *know* you want to join the approximately four million K–12 teachers currently employed in the United States—then you need to sort out your options. Becoming a teacher is a complicated process. This book provides you with the necessary information (or points you in the right direction to find it) so you can make the appropriate choices. Take a look at the following brief descriptions of what you will find in *Becoming a Teacher* to get an overview of how this book can help you.

**Chapter One** describes the many career options open to teachers. This will help narrow down your teaching career vision.

**Chapter Two** discusses a traditional teacher education program, the kinds of requirements that must be met, and how to choose a program. In addition, this chapter includes advice for those who may want an alternative route to teacher certification.

**Chapter Three** is an overview of paying for the teacher education programs in the United States.

**Chapter Four** deals with teacher certification requirements and examinations and provides contact information for the state boards of education, which handle certification.

**Chapters Five** and **Six** offer insight into how to get your first job and how to be successful there. You'll find the latest tips and techniques for conducting a job search and impressing your interviewers. Surviving that first year of teaching is also discussed—you'll get practice guidance on how to thrive in your new environment.

At the end of each chapter is a teacher profile. Some of these teachers are in their first or second year of teaching; others are more seasoned professionals. They teach in different areas of the country and at various levels. They tell you, in their own words, what teaching is all about.

Finally, appendixes provide more information to help you achieve your career goals. Appendix A is a list of professional organizations, which will be good resources as you enter the teaching field. Appendix B is a list of books and online resources that you can consult for more information about topics covered in this book. Appendix C will help you get familiar with the federal student aid (FAFSA) form.

# Becoming a
# TEACHER

# CHAPTER one

## DO YOUR CAREER HOMEWORK

**MANY CAREERS** are challenging, but few can provide the satisfaction that teaching does. The lessons that a teacher imparts can help propel his or her students toward future success. Education *appears* to consist of a single job—teaching. A closer look at the field, however, reveals that countless career opportunities exist.

This chapter introduces the many career options open to teachers: public and private schools, including charter schools; early childhood, elementary, middle, and secondary levels; and specialized areas, such as English as a Second Language (ESL), bilingual, and special education. Different certifications are required to teach at the early childhood, elementary, middle, and secondary level and for specific instructional areas that span kindergarten through grade 12 (commonly referred to as K–12). If you want to be a teacher, you will have to decide which age group of students you would like to work with and in which setting.

## TEACHERS IN EARLY AMERICA

Wanted Immediately: A Sober diligent Schoolmaster capable of teaching READING, WRITING, ARITHMETICK, and the Latin TONGUE . . . Any Person qualified as above, and well recommended, will be put into immediate Possession of the School, on applying to the Minister of Charles Parish, York County.

—*The Virginia Gazette*, August 20, 1772

The first American schools opened during the colonial era. When our country was still expanding, each new community built a schoolhouse—usually a one-room building—where children of all ages came to study together. Usually, one teacher, or schoolmaster, was responsible for teaching the children all the skills they needed to learn. The community took care of the teacher by providing housing and, sometimes, meals.

Schoolmasters were primarily male. In rural schools, teachers might also be farmers, surveyors, or innkeepers, who taught during their off-season. "Career" schoolmasters often used teaching as a stepping-stone to church or legal professions.

## THE EVOLVING JOB DESCRIPTION

A recent job posting for a teacher described the position as requiring someone who must be "responsible for providing an educational atmosphere where students have the opportunity to fulfill their potential for intellectual, emotional, physical, spiritual and psychological growth." Those are big shoes for one person to fill!

Traditionally, the role of a teacher was clearly defined *to instruct*. Today, the role is much more encompassing, because learning has become a larger part of our everyday lives. All children in the United States must, by law, attend school. Because 90% of today's fastest growing jobs require training or education beyond high school, more and more high school graduates go on to attend vocational schools, community colleges, or four-year colleges. People of all ages and from all walks of life continue their education throughout adulthood. In fact, the average person will have five careers in the course of a lifetime. Each career change requires "retooling"—that is, learning new skills—and each formal learning experience requires a teacher.

In the traditional model, it was assumed that the teacher had the information and that the teacher's job was to pass the information to the students. But teachers no longer only impart information; their job is to *facilitate learning*. This includes using a variety of teaching techniques, maintaining a safe and orderly classroom, developing lesson plans, assessing student progress, and interacting with members of the administration and community. To successfully play this role, teachers need an ever-expanding set of skills and knowledge to keep up with the needs of their students.

Teachers now teach children *how to learn*. Teachers not only motivate students to learn, but they teach them how to learn in a manner that is relevant, meaningful, and memorable. However, most educators agree that before they can do this, teachers' first job is to make students believe they can accomplish the task. This is done by building the students' self-esteem, often in one of the following ways:

- setting realistic student expectations
- creating classroom situations where students cannot fail
- developing innovative activities
- finding ways to give criticism in a positive manner
- keeping a record of successful activities

## IS TEACHING FOR YOU?

You say you want to be a teacher, but does the job suit you? To help you determine your answer, ask yourself these questions:

- Do I like working with children or young adults?
- Do I explain things well?
- Do I want to teach children or adults to appreciate their own worth?
- Do I have a solid command of the content I intend to teach?
- Am I inherently fair-minded?
- Am I a nurturing and encouraging person?
- Do I have a sense of humor?
- Am I a problem solver?
- Do I keep my cool in stressful situations?
- Do I rise to a challenge?
- Am I able to lead or follow, depending on the situation?
- Am I able to work with people, young or old, who might be difficult to get along with?

- Can I expand my direct assignment, working with the students, to include working with their families?
- Am I able to set expectations and hold people to those expectations?
- Am I detail-oriented?
- Do I manage time well?
- Do I want to feel tremendous personal reward and satisfaction at the end of my workday?

If you answered yes to most of these questions, then teaching is probably a very good choice for you. Every teacher interviewed for this book has similar sentiments about the rewards of the profession. In fact, not one teacher wanted to change his or her career path.

If you answered no to several of the preceding questions, think about what draws you to teaching. You really have to be a people person and a good problem solver to be a good classroom teacher.

But there are all kinds of related work you can do if the checklist above doesn't seem to apply to you. For instance, if you don't like to work with groups of people, think about a career as a reading or a resource room specialist, where you can work with students one at a time. If you want to teach because you love, say, English literature, think about teaching in a private academic high school or even a college, where you can indulge your scholarly side. There are many ways in which you can build a satisfying career in education, so make sure you find one that's right for you.

## WHY TEACHERS TEACH

Anyone who has ever referred to teaching as an easy job has obviously not spent a significant amount of time in an educator's shoes. Teaching can be physically and emotionally taxing as one deals with the problems of large classrooms, motivating and engaging today's students, or working with underinvolved parents or guardians. Teachers also have to balance their personal control over the classroom environment with external factors like administration demands or standardized testing.

Why would someone choose to teach, knowing that educators are faced with so many challenges? Most teachers believe that they make a difference in students' lives, and that is what makes teaching a rewarding and respected profession. Teachers are responsible for the education of future generations, which is no small feat. Another reward is that you will have a stimulating job that allows you to be a lifelong learner. Add to this the chance to work with interesting people from a variety of backgrounds and the ability to advocate for children and quality education—you can see why many people flock to this career!

Teacher Shana Ashwood explains, "I became a teacher because I have always admired the profession. To have a career where I could impact young lives on a daily basis by serving as a teacher, mentor, and role model was very appealing to me. I was specifically interested in working in a low socioeconomic community because I felt that was where I was most needed. While I was aware that teaching would have its share of challenges, it was the daily sense of accomplishment, the real-world relevance, and the opportunities for continued growth as a professional and as a member of the community that attracted me to the profession."

## FAMOUS AMERICANS WHO WERE ONCE TEACHERS

John Adams, president

Louisa May Alcott, author

Madeleine Albright, Secretary of
   State

Chester A. Arthur, president

Clara Barton, founder, American
   Red Cross

Alexander Graham Bell, inventor

Dan Brown, author

Sheryl Crow, singer/songwriter

Clarence Darrow, lawyer

Amelia Earhart, aviator

Geraldine Ferraro, vice
   presidential candidate

Abigail Fillmore, first lady

Roberta Flack, singer

Margaret Fuller, social reformer

Art Garfunkel, singer

Andy Griffith, actor

W. C. Handy, blues composer

Warren G. Harding, president

Edith Head, costume designer

Lyndon B. Johnson, president

Janis Joplin, rock star

Stephen King, author

Eugene McCarthy, senator

William McKinley, president

Herman Melville, author

James Michener, author

Anne Murray, singer

Carry Nation, temperance leader

Pat Nixon, first lady

Thomas Paine, patriot

General John Pershing,
   World War I leader

Susan Elizabeth Phillips, author

Lydia Pinkham, patent
   medicine manufacturer

Eleanor Roosevelt, first lady

Tim Russert, TV newscaster

Gene Simmons, musician

Mary Church Terrell, social reformer

Strom Thurmond, senator

## TEACHER SALARIES AND BENEFITS

Although it is true that few people will say that they went into teaching for the salary (many of these teachers' first professions began at higher starting salaries than most teaching jobs), *there is tremendous room for growth and extra income.*

### Median Salaries

The American Federation of Teachers (AFT) studied U.S. teachers' salaries and concluded there is a wide range both within and among states. Keep in mind that the salaries are as varied as the cost of living in each state. For example, it may cost you twice as much for housing in New York or California as it does in Alabama; the salaries reflect such differences. In fact, New York and California currently offer among the highest average teacher salaries.

The graph titled *Median Salary of K–12 Teachers* takes into account all K–12 teachers in the United States. For the average teacher, salaries are highest at the high school level.

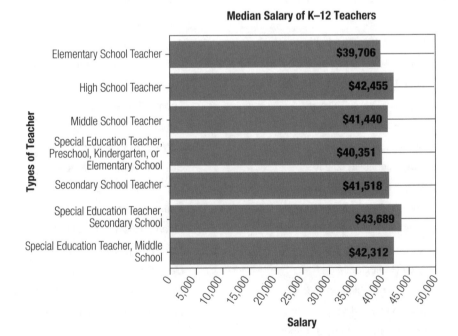

**Median Salary of K–12 Teachers**

| Types of Teacher | Salary |
| --- | --- |
| Elementary School Teacher | $39,706 |
| High School Teacher | $42,455 |
| Middle School Teacher | $41,440 |
| Special Education Teacher, Preschool, Kindergarten, or Elementary School | $40,351 |
| Secondary School Teacher | $41,518 |
| Special Education Teacher, Secondary School | $43,689 |
| Special Education Teacher, Middle School | $42,312 |

**Salary**

Remember that these are *salary ranges*. Some teachers earn more, and some earn less. And don't forget benefits. In addition to salary, most school districts pay into a retirement system and offer benefits such as medical insurance as part of the employment package.

## How Your Salary Grows

In teaching, years of experience make a difference. The second graph shows that the median starting salary for a teacher is around $34,000. Teachers employed in a public school setting are considered government employees. There are generally salary steps with yearly increments. In some districts, it may take 25 years to reach the top step. As you gain credit for each year, you move up the salary scale. It may take a few years for a teacher to move beyond this starting salary. However, after five or more years, the salary begins a steady increase.

Most districts also give you credit for courses completed. This benefit varies from district to district, but the concept is the same. As you continue your education and earn more credits, you earn more money. A master's

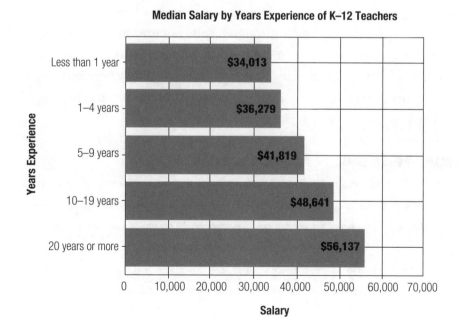

**Median Salary by Years Experience of K–12 Teachers**

degree, either an MA in education or a Master of Education degree, gives a teacher's salary a boost. In many districts, those with master's degrees make about twice as much as those with bachelor's degrees.

There is more good news. Teachers can earn additional money by helping with extracurricular or cocurricular activities. Departments need leadership, student council government needs supervision, teams needs coaches, and plays need directors. If you have a hobby that you'd like to share with students, maybe you can sponsor an after-school club. You can also help with after-school tutoring programs, administering and grading placement exams, or even teach summer school. Any of these activities adds to your base salary.

## HIRING TRENDS

Over the next ten years, many baby boomers will retire and leave teaching in large numbers. It's estimated that more than a million new teachers will be needed to replace them. In addition, hundreds of thousands of new teachers will be needed to keep pace with the anticipated growth of student populations.

The job market for teachers fluctuates by subject area, year, and geographical location. Because the U.S. government is placing a priority on education, there will be growth throughout the country in many educational areas. In fact, during his first Congressional address, President Barack Obama pledged to curb dropout rates, increase college-going rates, and improve teacher performance. He also promised to focus on merit-based pay for teachers, a system in which pay is based on performance.

### HOW RECESSION AFFECTS EDUCATION

Unfortunately, the worldwide recession of 2009 had a negative impact on school systems in some areas of the country. Some schools implemented hiring freezes, increased class sizes, and/or cut courses offerings. The impact on hiring new teachers was not estimated to last more than a few years, however.

On the positive side, President Obama's stimulus package included $115 billion in education aid, some of which will be used to prevent teacher cuts and layoffs.

There are about 14,000 school districts nationwide, and each local school board can determine which positions they want to add or delete. Sometimes, the size of a class is set by board policy or by contract. Therefore, as the community changes, so will the demographics of the school. Many suburban communities were developed as cities expanded. Young children needed schools, which were built to accommodate those needs. As the children grew and left home, the schools changed and, in many areas, were closed.

The Bureau of Labor Statistics' *Occupational Outlook Handbook* indicated that the job market for all teachers is growing at a rate as fast as the average for all other occupations with a 12% increase between 2006 and 2016. This increase will create about 479,000 additional teacher positions. Teacher candidates will have particularly good prospects in high-demand fields like math, science, and bilingual education, or in less desirable districts.

## TRY IT ON FOR SIZE

Teaching is not just a job. It is a *career* with a required path of education and expectations. You need to know what you are getting into before you begin. Once you have decided to make teaching your career, make arrangements to spend some time in a school and/or with students at the age you hope to teach.

One way to experience a classroom from a teacher's perspective is to go back to your own elementary, middle, or high school and ask to spend a day or an hour with a favorite teacher. If this is not possible, consider asking any teachers you know if you can observe their classroom for a day. If you have children in school or have friends who do, consider contacting the child's teacher.

If you are in high school, find out whether your school offers a cadet teaching program (through an organization such as Future Teachers of America or Future Teachers Association) that would allow you to teach carefully supervised lessons. You should also prepare for a college-level teacher education program by:

- challenging yourself with courses that get you ready for college-level work
- taking either the SAT or ACT

- researching where you will attend college
- considering what subject you would like to teach

Some community or four-year colleges offer programs that allow you to observe a teacher's classroom for a semester. For example, Rutgers University offers a course called "Exploring Teaching as a Profession," where one of the requirements is to spend a month in each an elementary and secondary classroom. Participants must observe both the teacher and students and are able to create their own lessons.

## Substitute Teaching

Another way to gain classroom experience before landing a teaching job is to substitute teach. Substituting is a wonderful opportunity to visit every grade level, allowing you to narrow down your classroom preferences. Spending time as a substitute teacher can help you to decide which teaching area to specialize in and which type of school district you'd like to work in.

In addition, substituting can be a nice source of income. Indeed, some substitute teachers in a mid to large city can earn $100 a day. Most states will allow you to become a substitute teacher if you have a bachelor's degree in any subject and if you meet their hiring procedures (some districts will do a background check, take your fingerprints, and want medical information). Some states will allow you to substitute teach even if you do not have a college degree, while others have more stringent requirements, which include passing a national teachers exam. Be sure to check your state's requirements by contacting your state education department.

Substitute teachers follow the school calendar, so you wouldn't work during school holidays and breaks, or during the summer. As a substitute, you get to choose which days you want to work and in which schools to take assignments. Once you are on a school district's list as an approved substitute teacher, you will get phone calls alerting you to an assignment—often early in the morning of the day they want you to teach. At the time of the phone call, you can say yes or no to the offer. However, if you say no more often than you say yes, you may find that you will get fewer offers in the future.

Some districts have automated calling systems in place, so you interact with a computer rather than a human.

Bridget Opfer graduated with a BA in Digital Arts and considered going back to school to become a teacher. To help make up her mind, she became a substitute teacher in her hometown, working with kids from second grade through high school. Bridget explains, "I knew teaching the students would give me a better idea of the subject and age of students I would like to teach. What I didn't count on, though, was how much I learned by watching other teachers in action. Because a lot of the classes were In Class Support (ICS), I was able to share the classroom with another experienced teacher. I was amazed to see how students responded to different teaching styles."

As unemployment rates continue to rise, there is a flood of applications for substitute teachers in all areas of the country. If you can obtain a substitute position, it's a valuable chance to pursue a career goal before you officially make your entry into a full-time teaching position. It also gets your teaching aspirations out there. As one teacher admits, "I had a lot of recommendations from other teachers I had been working with when I was substituting in local public schools. I think it was these recommendations that helped put me ahead of other candidates."

## CAREER CHANGERS WHO WANT TO BECOME TEACHERS

Many people are now entering the teaching field who previously held one or more jobs in other careers. In fact, one of the fastest-growing demographics among new teachers is career changers.

After eight years, Jennifer Kruter made the life-changing decision to leave the business world: "Working in corporate event marketing was unfulfilling. I wasn't doing anything to better the world around me. Through teaching, I can actually make a difference to the lives of my students. My goal in teaching is to challenge my students to think critically about the world around them—growing into active, engaged citizens within their own communities."

Due to the large demand for teachers in many areas, special programs have been created to recruit people from other occupations to become teachers. If you are considering changing careers to become a teacher, you've chosen a good time to make the switch due to the high demand for teachers. In the past decade, the number of teachers who obtained certification through an alternative route has increased dramatically. If you hold a bachelor's degree from an accredited college or university, you may be able to begin your teaching career as soon as you can apply for and land a job. Then, you can complete specific teacher education requirements while you are teaching. Many people are making this switch from another career to teaching.

## A SNAPSHOT OF THE DIFFERENT EDUCATIONAL SETTINGS

After you decide to enter the teaching profession, you now have to ask yourself where you want to live and work. You'll also need to consider where the job openings are.

### Choosing the Location

While the vast majority of teachers teach in public schools, you may also want to consider the possibility of teaching in a private school. A brief description of each setting will help you decide which one is more appropriate for you. Consider several factors before deciding whether to apply to teach in a public or a private school. First, private school salaries may or may not be comparable to those in the public schools. Public school salaries are normally presented on a salary schedule that reflects length of service and advanced degrees. You should inquire into private school salaries so you can compare beginning salaries and increases over a period of time and find out how the school remunerates for advanced degrees.

Another issue is job security. Some state laws allow districts to grant teachers tenure, often after three to five continuous years of service. Barring a serious decline in student enrollment or a serious breach of contract, you may reasonably expect continuous employment. In a private school, you may have to renew and renegotiate your salary and benefits each year. Regardless of whether they provide expectations for long-term employment or have salary schedules comparable to those of the public schools, private schools have other desirable factors to consider, such as the size of your class and the kind of student. Your talents and desires must match the education setting.

### Public Schools—Traditional and Charter Schools

In 2008, there were approximately 14,200 public school districts containing about 97,000 public schools, including about 4,000 charter schools. A public school system is open to all students who reside in a given community. Because the U.S. Constitution failed to mention education, the responsibility to provide a public education was established in state constitutions and defined by state laws. The money to run the schools comes from local, state, and federal government. Therefore, the government supervises almost all functions of the school—curriculum, teacher certification, special education programs, vocational programs, test scores, school attendance, and teacher tenure.

Every state has established a department of education that supervises education within the state and serves as a liaison between the local district and the federal government. This department ensures that the school year has the required number of days in attendance (typically between 175 and 185 days). Each state has a recommended or required curriculum, and a statewide assessment is usually administered at several grade levels. Some states require students to pass exit examinations in grade 12 before they can be awarded diplomas. In fact, by 2012, 74% of the nation's public school students will be required to pass an exit exam to graduate, according to a 2008 report released by the Washington, DC-based Center on Education Policy. Finally, the state department of education accredits a district's or a school's program so that teachers, parents or guardians, and students can rest assured that their school district or school meets certain quality standards.

## CHARTER SCHOOLS

The charter school, which is picking up momentum in many states, is a type of public school that offers specialized programs and smaller classes. President Barack Obama supports the charter school expansion as part of his effort to reform U.S. education.

Many charter schools have atypical grade configurations (e.g., K–3 or K–8). A charter school is usually governed by a group or organization under a contract or charter with the state. The charter excuses the school from certain state or local rules and regulations. Parents and guardians, community leaders, businesses, teachers, school districts, or municipalities can start a charter school.

In return for public funding and freedom, the charter school must meet accountability standards. A school's charter is reviewed every three to five years and can be revoked if curriculum and management guidelines are not followed or the accountability standards are not met.

Some teachers choose to teach in charter schools because of the schools' innovative approaches to education, their high academic standards, small class size, or because the charter school's educational philosophies are in line with their own.

Charter schools vary a lot from state to state and school to school, so if you are interested in teaching in a charter school, do some research on those that are available in your area. To find out more about charter schools and to find links to a list of charter schools in your state, visit the U.S. Charter Schools website at www.uscharterschools.org.

In 2008, approximately 49.8 million students attended public schools. Of these, 34.9 million were in prekindergarten through grade 8 and 14.9 million were in grades 9 through 12.

In 2008, public schools employed about 3.3 million teachers. Public school teachers are usually state certified or working toward certification, which ensures that they have gone through the training required by the state. This includes student teaching and specific coursework. The federal statutes under No Child Left Behind (NCLB) require a minimum of bachelor's degree for all public school teachers.

### Private Schools

In 2008, there were about 35,000 private schools offering kindergarten or higher grades. Private schools may be similar to public schools educationally, but one major difference exists: Private schools do not receive funding from state or federal sources. Therefore, they do not have to follow all the same rules and regulations as the public schools. Each private school operates independently, but its curriculum must be approved by the state department of education. However, they are not subject to the limitations of state education budgets and have more freedom in designing curriculum and instruction.

Private schools may be endowed or supported by a religious affiliation. They usually charge tuition, which may be substantial. However, parochial schools, which enroll more students than any other segment of private schools, often charge less. Some schools offer student scholarships, and some have flexible tuition policies.

A private school has a unique student population, because it can accept or refuse admission to students, whereas public schools must take in all residents within the district.

Many private schools' education programs prepare the students for college. Some offer a classical education, rather than the traditional liberal arts education offered in most public schools; these schools prepare students for elite U.S. colleges and universities. Military schools demand academic achievement along with physical training and strict discipline. Other schools may have an exploratory philosophy or specialize in a unique type of child, such as gifted youngsters. Teachers in these environments must follow the program set up by the school. Staff members may have special training or hold advanced degrees.

Private religious schools offer basic education in mathematics, science, communication arts, social studies, and all other subjects required by the state. Religious instruction and practice supplement this traditional program. Religious schools differ from other private schools because they attract students who usually, but not always, have a similar religious affiliation.

## CATHOLIC SCHOOLS

Currently, there are approximately 7,498 Catholic schools: 6,288 elementary/middle and 1,210 secondary. If you want to find out more about teaching in a Catholic private school, contact the National Catholic Education Association or visit their web site at http://www.ncea.org. If you'd like to investigate on your own, take a look at the U.S. cities with the most Catholic schools and largest student enrollments:

| | |
|---|---|
| Baltimore | New Orleans |
| Boston | New York |
| Chicago | Philadelphia |
| Cincinnati | Pittsburgh |
| Cleveland | Rockville Centre, N.Y. |
| Detroit | St. Louis |
| Los Angeles | St. Paul/Minneapolis |
| Miami | San Francisco |
| Milwaukee | Washington, D.C. |
| Newark | |

In 2008, approximately 6.2 million students attended private schools and 0.5 million teachers worked in these schools.

For private school teachers, certification may not be required. Instead, these teachers often possess subject area expertise and an undergraduate or graduate degree in the subject they teach.

## City, Town, or Country

Sharp differences exist among urban, suburban, and rural school districts. Your happiness in the teaching profession may be severely affected by where you decide to teach.

### Urban Schools

Urban schools have been adversely affected by the changing demographics in this country. Middle-class flight from the city has decreased the tax base necessary to adequately pay teachers, maintain facilities, and provide appropriate and current resources.

Teaching in an urban school is a unique and demanding challenge. Students in urban schools tend to be more ethnically diverse and more likely to be affected by low socioeconomic factors than their rural and suburban counterparts. Also, many students in urban districts start school with fewer of the skills they need to be successful. Achievement gaps are widening, and the need for well-qualified teachers in urban schools has never been greater.

Urban districts tend to have a large bureaucracy and centralized control. This organizational structure decreases your flexibility as a teacher in the classroom. Teachers typically follow a district-adopted curriculum and use district-adopted materials in their classrooms. In addition, many inner-city parents and guardians feel disenfranchised from the school system and therefore do not actively participate in their children's education.

Despite these problems, many teachers in urban districts find their jobs very satisfying. Urban or inner-city schools often provide a wonderful opportunity for beginning teachers because more jobs are available in a large district.

## Suburban Schools

Suburban school districts have boomed since the urban flight of the late 1950s and 1960s. These districts tend to have more money to spend on education than rural or urban districts and therefore have newer facilities, smaller class sizes, and more class resources and materials. Parents and guardians tend to be actively involved in the school and very demanding of both teachers and administrators. Traditionally, the suburban district had a rather homogeneous student body, but that population is changing as suburban communities become more racially and ethnically diverse.

## A TEACHER'S HOURS

As a teacher, your day doesn't necessarily begin and end when the school bell rings. Generally, teachers arrive at school prior to students in order to prepare for the day. After school, you may be involved in after-school meetings or committees, helping students, grading homework, creating assignments and projects, or calling parents or guardians.

During the summer break, many teachers still work—teaching summer school or participating in professional development conferences, trainings, or fellowships in order to increase their skills and knowledge.

All these demands require a willingness to sacrifice what in other professions is considered personal time.

## Rural Schools

Rural school districts tend to have smaller student populations, fewer resources, and fewer opportunities than their urban and suburban counterparts. Reflections of rural America, they also tend to be more conservative (socially and politically) and more racially and ethnically homogeneous. Some believe that rural schools are safer than urban or suburban districts. The rural community is very family-oriented, as many students live on farms, which also promotes a strong work ethic. Rural teachers typically have more control over what is taught in the classroom and which materials are selected for their classes.

## Areas of Specialization

Choosing what to teach is probably the most important question you need to ask yourself. What age students would you enjoy teaching? What subjects can you visualize yourself teaching? If you think you would like to teach a variety of subjects, you might be a good candidate for elementary-age students, a position often referred to as a generalist. If you prefer to specialize in a subject like computers or Spanish, you might be a good fit for middle school or high school students.

Here's a look at several different areas you can choose to specialize in as a teacher. Keep in mind that you may be able to combine some of these areas of specialization. For example, you can become certified as a high school teacher in science and also gain certification in special education. Or perhaps you want to become an elementary school teacher in a bilingual classroom. To compete for the best jobs in the best school districts, or to advance your salary level, you may want to obtain certifications in one, two, or more of these areas.

## Early Childhood Education

If you enjoy working with very young children, you may want to become an early childhood education teacher. Early childhood education programs (often referred to as prekindergarten, or PK) are for 3- and 4-year-olds; however, some special education PK programs include children from birth to age 5. In addition to teaching opportunities in public schools, a wide variety of private schools run by religious organizations, hospitals, colleges, and large corporations also have openings for qualified teachers.

As an early childhood educator, you would select, create, and plan age-appropriate activities to help students develop motor skills, counting skills, and literacy skills. Your day would have a lot of variety due to the limited attention span of very young children. Activities include small group art projects, large group story times, outside play, nap time, meals and snacks, quiet-time games, and creative play.

When asked to explain the biggest reward as an early childhood educator, one retired teacher exclaimed, "The children, of course! I started out as a science teacher for grades PK–3. As an early childhood science teacher, I had a unique opportunity to cultivate the sense of wonder, interest, and excitement that children naturally have at that age. Everything to them is new and exciting. Children have a lot of questions about the world and it's exciting to witness when they discover the answers!"

Early childhood education has become a hot topic. In 2009, President Obama pledged to increase funding for early childhood education. In his policy paper titled "Early Childhood Development: Economic Development with a High Public Return," coauthor and economist Rob Grunewald stated that 85% of children's brains are developed by the time they are 3 years old. "Because of that, the environment in early years is so impactful to children, [and] we believe investments should be made in those early years," he says.

Check with your state department of education to see if they offer a certificate in early childhood education. Additionally, you can earn certification from the National Child Care Association as a Certified Childcare Professional. For more information, visit the National Child Care Association's website at www.nccanet.org.

### Elementary School

The elementary level usually includes kindergarten and a grade between third and sixth. In districts where kindergarten is included, it can be on a half-day or full-day schedule. Sometimes, the elementary school has been further divided in a primary school (grades K–2 or PK–2) and an upper or intermediate school (grades 3–6). Many districts have adopted a middle school philosophy in which grade 6 (and sometimes grade 5) is housed in the middle school.

### Regular Elementary Education

The elementary license usually covers grades K–6, sometimes K–8. Elementary school teachers are generalists who must be prepared to teach science, social studies, mathematics, and language arts. Art, music, physical education, library science, and technology may be part of their responsibility, or specialty teachers may handle these areas. Elementary school teachers also must be prepared to accurately diagnose learning problems: A developmental problem will disappear, with additional help, as the student matures; however, a student who is disabled will require extra attention from special education teachers.

In some elementary schools, all teachers on a grade level have the same conference period, so they can plan instruction collaboratively. Others are departmentalized, so a teacher who is interested in and prefers math and science may teach math and science to all the second graders and another teacher may handle the reading and language arts instruction. Also, you can move within up to seven grade levels (depending on how the district is organized) in an elementary school. For example, if you would like a change from the curriculum you teach and want variety, you can switch from grade 1 to grade 4 if an opening exists and the principal approves it.

Teaching at the elementary level provides great satisfaction. Children grow up before your eyes. They stay in your school for five to seven years, and their older and younger siblings often know who you are. In the classroom with these youngsters every day, you become like a family for a year. You take your students on field trips, catch their colds, and worry with them about everything. Teachers can become very attached to their students, and that bond is wonderful and enriching. Some of your former students will even come back to visit you many years later due to the strength of a warm relationship.

Parent and guardian participation varies quite a bit, of course, but elementary school is the level at which most families are involved with their children's education. Positive interaction with parents and guardians can support and reward your efforts in the classroom, but it is also very time-consuming. In a large urban setting, you may become frustrated because the children have more problems and fewer involved parents or guardians. In a rural or suburban district, where parental involvement and support are high, you may be expected to attend evening meetings with parents and guardians, as well as numerous PTA functions.

As an elementary teacher, you spend the entire day with your class, which can be exhausting. Although you are given a planning period and time to eat lunch, the bulk of your day is spent with young people, who can be very demanding. You have very little interaction with other adults during the day, yet you must be able to cooperate with specialized teachers—the reading specialist, the art teacher, and so on—who are involved with students in your class. You must be able to work with children at different levels of development and from many different backgrounds, and you have to teach every subject that the state requires. All of this can add up to a demanding work schedule.

Even if you prefer a specific grade level in the K–6 school, you are likely to be placed wherever there is an opening for you that first year. Remember, as the new teacher in the school, you may have to take on the type of assignments that the teachers with more seniority don't necessarily prefer. Teaching any of the elementary grades will give you tremendous experience, even if you are teaching 10–year-olds when you actually prefer to build a career teaching first grade and specialize in reading. Chances are, if you perform well with the classroom you are given, your preferences will be taken into consideration as you build tenure at your school.

## Primary Education

Primary education is offered as a separate license from elementary education in some states, giving you the chance to specialize in one of the following grade levels:

- prekindergarten
- kindergarten
- grade 1
- grade 2
- grade 3

Primary education is similar to elementary education, but the young ages of the children make for unique challenges that a fifth or sixth grade teacher in an elementary school would not have to face.

At first glance, many people think primary education is easy, but this level can be the most challenging one in the system. If you are considering a specialty in primary education, visit a kindergarten or first grade class for a day—just for a quick reality check. It takes a special kind of person to organize these youngsters and to give them the tools to learn—first to read and then to find the information they need. Primary teachers often have to teach children how to put on and take off their coats, never mind reading, writing, and arithmetic.

Picture this: It is the first day of school. Your class consists of 4- and 5-year-olds. Some of them are very nervous about being away from home. One or two might be clinging to a parent, not willing to let go. Children may be crying—moms and dads, too. Your job is to line up the children to bring them into your classroom. You announce, "Line up, please," and nobody pays attention. The concept of lining up needs to be taught—forget about the first alphabet lesson! Some children even forget they are toilet trained, and others spill their lunches all over your new sweater. And to complicate events further, a few parents and guardians have decided to videotape this occasion for posterity.

Within a few days, however, the students are all seated at desks, learning letters, numbers, and your name—the magic has begun! In grade 1, you are expected to teach students to read, write, and compute as well as set up a pattern of learning that will stay with them forever. Primary grade teachers may be the most influential people in the child's educational career, and a strong beginning is most important to a strong education. The process of learning in a classroom setting often begins in the primary grades (for children who have not previously participated in early childhood education). Arguably, first grade teachers have the toughest job. With that said, it may be the most rewarding, as well. Few milestones are as memorable for student, parent, and teacher than learning to read. Watch a first grade teacher unravel the mystery of language with a class of children. One by one, students figure out the code, and the reading process begins. This is truly an exciting time in the classroom and a great moment for the teacher.

The early primary grades are also physically demanding on teachers. Ask physical education teachers, who are on their feet all day long, which classes are the most tiring. Most will say kindergarten. In the beginning, teachers have to do everything for the children, rendering educating secondary to the role of disciplinarian, babysitter, and nurse. Most primary grade teachers will tell you to save your best and most fragile clothing for the weekend—the hands-on teaching required often means getting your hands, and clothing, dirty.

## TEACHING OUTSIDE THE BOX

Once you have decided to become a teacher, get involved in activities with children. For example, you can

- volunteer at the local YMCA, YWCA, a Girls or Boys Club, or another community agency that provides after-school programs for children.
- intern in a nursery school or daycare center.
- tutor a child in your neighborhood.
- volunteer as a tutor at a local school.
- be a camp counselor for your community, church, or synagogue.
- babysit for your relatives.

Any of these activities will provide excellent experience by giving you a chance to put your learning into action while strengthening your skills (and your resume).

## MIDDLE SCHOOL OR JUNIOR HIGH SCHOOL

The middle level teaching certification and/or licenses cover grades between 4 and 9. The exact grades covered vary from state to state, as seen in the table.

## Certification/Licensure Patterns by State

| State | License Type | Grade Levels | State | License Type | Grade Levels |
|---|---|---|---|---|---|
| Alabama | License | 4–8 | Kentucky | License | 5–9 |
| Alaska | Endorsement | 5–8 | Louisiana | Endorsement | 4–8 |
| Arizona | Endorsement | 5–9 | Maine | Endorsement | 5–8 |
| Arkansas | License | 4–8 | Maryland | License | 4–9 |
| California | None | None | Massachusetts | License | 5–9 |
| Colorado | None | None | Michigan | Endorsement | 5–9 |
| Connecticut | License | 5–9 | Minnesota | License | 5–8 |
| Delaware | License | 5–9 | Mississippi | Endorsement | 4–8 |
| District of Columbia | License | 5–8 | Missouri | License | 5–8 |
| Florida | Endorsement | 5–9 | Montana | None | None |
| Georgia | License | 4–8 | Nebraska | Endorsement | 4–9 |
| Hawaii | License | 5–9 | Nevada | License | 7–9 |
| Idaho | None | None | New Hampshire | License | 5–8 |
| Illinois | Endorsement | 5–8 | New Jersey | Endorsement | 5–8 |
| Indiana | License | 5–8 | New Mexico | Endorsement | 5–8 |
| Iowa | Endorsement | 5–8 | New York | Endorsement | 5–9 |
| Kansas | License | 5–8 | North Carolina | License | 6–9 |

*(continued)*

## Certification/Licensure Patterns by State *(continued)*

| State | License Type | Grade Levels | State | License Type | Grade Levels |
|---|---|---|---|---|---|
| North Dakota | License | 5–8 | Texas | License | 4–8 |
| Ohio | License | 4–9 | Utah | License | 5–9 |
| Oklahoma | Endorsement | 4–8 | Vermont | License | 5–8 |
| Oregon | License | 5–9 | Virginia | License | 6–8 |
| Pennsylvania | License | 4–8 | Washington | Endorsement | 5–9 |
| Rhode Island | Endorsement | 5–8 | West Virginia | License | 5–9 |
| South Carolina | License | 5–8 | Wisconsin | License | 5–9 |
| South Dakota | License | 5–8 | Wyoming | License | 5–8 |
| Tennessee | License | 5–8 | | | |

**Note:** *License* is used to indicate that a separate middle level license is available. *Endorsement* is used when the middle level teaching license is available only as an add-on credential for those also qualifying for a different license.)

Traditionally, students entered the junior high school after grade 6 to complete grades 7 and 8, and sometimes 9; and the junior high school was a small version of the high school. Students followed a schedule and subject matter similar to those of the high school. The newer middle school concept has been adopted in many districts. Middle schools usually house grades 6–8 (sometimes 9) and are organized on the belief that students in these grades are unique and need opportunities, beyond purely academic pursuits, to explore vocational and avocational interests. Students are offered "exploratories" that expose them to many interesting intellectual or social/emotional activities. Middle school schedules often are built on blocks of time that can be manipulated to provide longer periods for certain activities during the school day. Additionally, teachers are organized into teams, so a group of students shares the same teachers in the core curriculum areas. The team teachers meet periodically to discuss the intellectual, emotional, and social needs of the students. For more information about middle schools, visit the National Middle School Association's website at www.nmsa.org.

## High School

High schools house grades 9–12, or 10–12, depending on the district. A few districts group grade 9 in the middle or junior high school, and some house the ninth grade separately. The schedule of the high school day may vary. Traditionally, the school day was divided into six or seven 45- to 60-minute teaching periods. Today, some high schools have block schedules that divide the school day into as few as four periods or as many as ten or more periods. Some schools, such as one in San Juan High School in California, are adventurous enough to offer their students schedules in both traditional and block formats.

## Middle, Junior, or High School Subject Specialties

If you love a particular subject, then you may want to choose a subject area to specialize in at the middle school, junior high school, or high school level. Are you a history buff who knows every battle from the Civil War? Do you love to read and find yourself trying to encourage others to read with you? Are you very good in math? Do you have a mechanical mind and love working on your car? If you want to become an expert in one field and share your passion with your students, teaching at the secondary level may be for you. There are many different subject areas you can select, such as:

- English and language arts
- mathematics
- physical education
- health
- social studies
- music
- art
- drama
- sciences
- computers

- home economics
- technical and vocational education
- education media

Schools keep adding more departments, and each one has subspecialties within the broad scope of the curriculum. The license for many of the academic departments commonly found in middle school, junior high school, and high school is usually for grades 7–12. Licenses for music, art, and physical education are often K–12. Certification requirements vary by state, but each specialty requires a separate license.

With a subject area specialization, you could teach five variations of a subject within a department or, if it is needed, you could repeat the same class four times to different groups of students. You may be asked to teach a class that is not in your subject area (and if you are new, you must say yes). Some teachers thrive in this kind of environment, rewarded by the opportunity to delve into a subject and to share their interest in that subject with many different students.

### Special Education

Special education is a demanding, yet rewarding, area of specialization that is growing by leaps and bounds. In 2009, President Obama's economic stimulus package more than doubled current federal funding for special education programs. The number needed is expected to increase by 15% by 2016—faster than the average for all occupations. Increases in the number of special education students will generate a greater need for special education teachers. So, if you have a soft spot in your heart for children with special needs, consider making this your specialty.

The range of possibilities in this area is vast. The special education license is usually very broad, covering grades K–12. If you have this certification, a school district can place you in any number of settings. You can even work in a residential setting if impaired students are too disabled to come to a general education building. Most public schools house their own special education classes, but this is not always the case.

There are, of course, many types of disabilities. Whenever possible, students with disabilities are mainstreamed into a regular classroom for all or part of their school day. Students with many kinds of physical disabilities, for instance, can learn right along with the regularly abled students of their same age. However, other kinds of disabilities may require that students get special support, either part-time out of the regular classroom or in a special class. Depending on your state, you may be able to get a special license to handle, for instance, students who are visually impaired, students with orthopedic disabilities, children with behavioral disorders, and many others.

Special education teachers may work alone or with others to create Individualized Education Programs (IEPs) for each of their students. An IEP is a written agreement between the parents or guardians and the school about what each child needs and what will be done to address those needs; IEPs are mandated by a federal law called the Individuals with Disabilities Education Act (IDEA).

Children classified as "learning disabled" often have equal or better natural intelligence than other students in the school; they just have a problem in the processing. They fall under federal special education laws, and teachers must follow an IEP for each one of them. While there is some room for creativity, the plan must be fully implemented.

## SPECIAL EDUCATION CATEGORIES

While the areas of specialization within the broad heading of special education vary significantly from state to state, here is a list of several categories of special needs:

- attention deficit disorder
- at-risk children
- autism
- blind
- deaf
- deaf-blind
- developmentally delayed
- hard of hearing
- mental retardation: mild/moderate
- mental retardation: severe/profound
- multiply disabled
- orthopedic impairments
- other health impairments
- serious emotional disturbance
- specific learning disabilities

- speech or language impairments
- traumatic brain injury
- visually impaired
- cross-categorical
- noncategorical

A special education license allows you to teach children with varied needs. For a student with a serious disability, you may be the one person who helps integrate the special education student into society. Motivating children who have disabilities to succeed often requires tremendous patience and energy. These children may need more repetitive teaching strategies or more intensive assistance, such as being accompanied to the bathroom or physically moved from place to place. The degree of these challenges varies among the subspecialty areas. Special education requires a deep commitment. If you like to help others in addition to teaching them, this is an excellent area of education for you. For more information about issues in special education, contact the Council for Exceptional Children's website at www.cec.sped.org.

## Concentrations in Special Education

Most teacher education programs prepare you for a special education license that allows you to work with many different disabilities. However, some teacher education programs offer *concentrations* of courses in one of the specialized areas that follow.

**Resource Room.** Students who need support in a particular deficit area may be taken out of their regular classroom for several hours a week to study with a small group. Teaching in a resource room, you work with children who spend most of their day in a regular classroom but require modified instruction. Resource room teachers sometimes work as consultants for the students in the regular classroom with another instructor. **Self-Contained Classroom.** Every school district has a different method of assigning students to a self-contained classroom. The class may include children with different problems, only children with physical disabilities, or only children with emotional or learning disabilities. As teacher of a self-contained classroom, you probably spend most of the day with the same class. Classes are sometimes cross-graded, and you may have a teacher's aide assisting you. The class size may be up to, but cannot exceed, 15 students.

**Visually Impaired.** As a teacher of visually impaired students, you may work in a school that specializes in this area or within a regular education setting, one-on-one or with small groups. You would prepare special materials for the students, help other instructors modify programs, and you would probably need to know Braille. You may need a specialized license to work with visually impaired students in some states.

**Hearing Impaired.** Hearing-impaired children who need special services may be in a regular classroom setting or in a school that specializes in this area. As a teacher of hearing-impaired students, you probably would need to know sign language and would help full-time classroom teachers modify their programs for your students. Working with students who are hearing impaired requires a specialized license in some states.

**Physically Disabled.** Some students cannot do any physical tasks on their own; they must be fed, bathed, and tended to during the day by school staff. These children, from infants to age twenty-one, may have full-time nurses and very serious physical limitations that make them unable to attend regular public schools. Their classes generally are held away from the regular classrooms because of the students' special physical needs.

## Reading Specialist

To make yourself more marketable, you may want to obtain a license in reading in addition to either regular education or special education. This license offers flexibility in K–12 assignments. The job is varied and interesting. As a reading specialist, you may work with gifted students or with students who have fallen behind. Some reading teachers work as *teacher trainers*, helping other staff members. Other reading teachers work with the school's administration to develop standardized reading programs for that school. You may get the chance to organize reading clubs and contests, book fairs, or special visits from authors of children's books.

Each district has its own standards and regulations about how reading teachers are used. The bottom line is that this license can help you get a job, especially if you use it to support a regular education or special educatio license. For more information, visit the International Reading Association's website at www.reading.org.

### Bilingual Education

This area of specialization requires that you be *fluent in a language in addition to English*. You teach limited-English proficient (LEP) students subject matter in their native tongue while they learn to speak English. In New York City, for example, there are bilingual classes in Russian, Farsi, Korean, Japanese, Chinese, Spanish, Creole, and other languages. Bilingual teachers mostly work in elementary schools and middle schools. In the past, bilingual educators were needed mainly in large urban areas in California, Texas, and New York. However, the number of limited-English-proficient students is now increasing in other school districts (South Carolina, Arkansas, Indiana, North Carolina, and Tennessee), so opportunities for bilingual educators are increasing all across the nation. Due to the severe lack of qualified bilingual teachers, several federal, state, and local programs have been created to help people obtain teacher training and certification in bilingual education. To get more information about bilingual education, visit the National Clearinghouse for Bilingual Education's website at www.ncbe.gwu.edu.

### English as a Second Language

As an English as a Second Language (ESL) teacher, you *do not have to speak another language*. Using specialized techniques, you work with small groups of students—who may speak any number of foreign languages—to teach them English. Often, your students change throughout the day, coming to you from their regular or bilingual classrooms for a few hours of ESL work every day. You may have the help of one or more teacher aides who speak the language of the students you are teaching. However, this is not always the case.

eachers are needed at all the levels: prekindergarten, elementary, ool, junior high school, and high school. Many states require that be provided for several years. Children who are born in the but live in a house where English is not spoken can be eligible . For more information, visit the Teachers of English to r Languages (TESOL) website at www.tesol.org.

## Physical Education

If you love to play sports and take part in other physical activities, you may be interested in pursuing a career as a physical education teacher. Physical education teachers at the elementary and high school levels have very different roles to fulfill. For example, if you want to become a physical education teacher in an elementary school, you would focus on helping your students to develop motor skills and to play organized games together. Running games are popular at this level. You may need to teach at more than one elementary school if each school has limited physical education requirements for their students (some schools offer gym classes only once or twice a week).

If you choose to teach physical education at the middle school or junior high school level, you will probably teach six or seven different classes each day. You may specialize in one area, such as sports, health, or dance or rotate areas throughout the school year. In high schools, physical education teachers may teach students a variety of team and individual sports, including swimming, weight training, and gymnastics. You will most likely be encouraged to become a coach for one or more sports activities that take place after regular school hours—and you will get additional pay for each coaching assignment. If you get intensely involved in extracurricular team sports, you may spend a lot of time traveling to other schools and cities for games, competitions, and tournaments. For more information, visit the National Association for Sport and Physical Education's website at www.aahperd.org/naspe.

## Music Education

If you've always loved music or are a musician, you could bring your passion to students and learning. One teacher explains, "It's also really interesting to present a rather complex musical idea to a child and find that it is not so complex to a child, with a young, absorbent mind, ready to soak up the world." As a teacher specializing in music, several opportunities are available to you, including band teacher, choral teacher, and orchestra teacher.

Similar to physical education teachers in elementary schools, you may need to teach music classes in more than one school per day. That is because students often attend music class only once or twice a week at this level. In these situations, teachers have to adjust rapidly to different age groups, which can sometimes be difficult when an eighth grade class follows a kindergarten. The subject matter and level of proficiency of the two age groups are so different that it is sometimes hard to switch gears.

In addition, interacting with classroom teachers can take some practice. Sharing lessons and ideas, especially when other teachers see your class as secondary to the core subjects (reading, writing, math, and so on) that they teach, can be a challenge. The best way to manage this relationship is to follow what the classroom teachers are teaching and adapt your music lessons to fit in with their subject matter. For example, if the students are studying antebellum history, try teaching folk ballads, spirituals, and patriotic songs from that period. This strategy helps engage the students as they began to make connections between the classroom materials and the music as primary resources.

Your duties as an elementary school music teacher would include introducing young children to the history and rhythms of music and guiding children in singing activities. In older elementary grades, students are often encouraged to join choirs or begin playing a musical instrument.

If you choose to become a music teacher at the middle school level, you will probably spend time teaching students basic music appreciation and choral singing, as well as guiding bands or orchestras. You may sponsor or organize special concerts throughout the year in which your students perform for the public.

At the high school level, music teachers teach regular classes in different types of music, just like the other high school teachers teach classes in their subject area. However, many music teachers have duties after regular school hours, such as directing student bands, orchestras, and chorals for plays, sports events, and concerts. For more information on music education careers, visit the National Association for Music Education's website at www.menc.org.

### Computers/Technology Education

Technology is taught in grades K–12. In grades 6–12, it is taught as a subject by certified technology teachers, and in grades K–5 teachers may incorporate technology concepts into other subjects.

Teachers who specialize in computers or technology education often manage a resource room that contains computers or some other type of computer lab in their school. They may focus on training both students and teachers in the use of computers—helping teachers to integrate the use of technology into their lessons and helping students to learn how to use computers. The level of expertise varies among teachers in the computer/technology area. Some have a background in computer hardware and software and do the actual maintenance and troubleshooting of the school's computers, while others may have a more managerial role, assigning repairs to someone else. Nonteaching duties for computer/technology specialists vary from school to school, but you may be expected to manage equipment budgets, design or update school web pages, and develop new technology plans or programs. Teaching duties in a computer lab may include coaching small groups of students, leading a full class, or coteaching different subjects with another teacher. For more information, visit the International Technology Education Association website at www.iteaconnect.org.

If you are still undecided about your preferred teaching location, level, or area of specialization when you enroll in a teacher education program, don't panic. Not all of your choices will be obvious at the outset, and you don't have to decide right away. Most programs offer opportunities to observe or volunteer in classrooms early on, long before the student teaching assignment.

## THE INSIDE TRACK

| | |
|---|---|
| Who: | Mona H. Ford |
| What: | High School English Teacher |
| Where: | Hillcrest High School, Memphis, Tennessee |
| Type of School: | Urban Public School |
| | |
| How long: | 25 years as teacher and trainer |
| Degree(s): | BS in Education, 1979; 15 years toward ME in Curriculum and Instructional Design |
| School: | University of Memphis |

### Insider's Advice

Love what you do. No matter how the day ends, if you love teaching, you can come back the next day. Experience has taught me that one never knows the immediate impact of an endeavor. Sometimes we find out years later, in special and unexpected ways.

### What I Wish I Had Learned in School

The capacity to learn something, and then to apply it, was never addressed in school when I attended. I never understood why reading all those books in high school would be so important. I came up in a generation where being able to read was considered a treasure in itself, so I was taught to appreciate and love it. The practical application of such a great skill was never addressed, although I benefited greatly from having received such a great education.

### Greatest Joy

This goes back to the power of discovery when I realize that I have had a tremendous influence when I thought, at the time, that my efforts were futile. I love having my students return and thank me for helping them become successful. Since parents and guardians have virtually left their high-school-aged children for teachers and others to raise and influence, we cannot gauge the impact of our efforts until our students leave us and discover the gifts that we have given them.

### Biggest Drawback

There is a huge disconnect between the reality of the classroom environment and how administrators and parents or guardians perceive this. This creates many support problems for teachers. I always feel saddled with more and more responsibility and *paperwork*, with less authority and pay.

### Future Plans

Undecided. Maybe I will teach for one more year, but I will definitely publish something in the next two years. I have been haphazardly working on a book about my mother and another on family history, which I have been researching since 1984. I have had the opportunity to travel throughout Europe and to four of the seven continents. I also plan to add some more travel miles to my portfolio, especially return trips to Alaska and Washington, DC.

# CHAPTER two

## ALL ABOUT TEACHER EDUCATION PROGRAMS

**MANY STEPS** are involved in becoming a teacher. The first one is to get the proper training. You must select a school that will meet the future demands of your profession. This chapter explains the requirements common to most teacher education programs in the United States.

Before you can begin your career as a teacher, you must acquire the necessary education. The good news is that many routes exist for you to get the teaching education you need. Depending on your current educational background, this could mean: obtaining a four-year college degree from an accredited teacher education program; or, if you already hold a college degree but it isn't in the education field, you can enroll in a teacher education graduate program; or you may only need to take a few specific education courses at an institution approved by your state department of education. Another option available to you is distance learning, which enables you to learn in your own home at your own pace.

While you have to complete a certain amount of teacher education in order to become certified as a teacher, you don't always need to obtain your full certification in order to land your first full-time teaching job. This is especially true in urban or rural areas where there is often a high demand for teachers.

No matter what your situation is—a high school student just starting out, a two- or four-year college student who has decided to go into teaching, or a college graduate deciding to change careers—you have to complete a teacher education program in order to be certified as a teacher. If you want to begin teaching immediately after college, without obtaining a graduate degree, you must attend a school that offers a program in your interest area that ensures you have the necessary educational credentials to obtain certification. If you want to study something more esoteric in your undergraduate years and still be able to teach, you can get a graduate degree with a concentration in education. Either way, you must have *specialized training in education* to obtain certification, get hired, and become a successful teacher.

## CHANGES IN TEACHER EDUCATION

Several major changes in both theory and practice have turned the traditional classroom into a more exciting learning environment. These changes include new instructional materials, technology, and understandings of how children learn. These elements have changed the way teachers instruct students, and the training program you select should provide you with information and opportunities to experience these changes.

### Instructional Materials

Just a few years ago, every student had a textbook, and every teacher had a teacher's edition of that book and maybe a workbook for reinforcement. Using a formal lesson plan, teachers would assign a chapter to read on Monday, provide several worksheets to complete and grade in class during the week, and then give a chapter test on Friday.

Today, teachers still use textbooks, but the books come with kits containing multiple resources such as videos, laser discs, and software to use in their classrooms. There is a broad range of instructional material available, which can be classified in seven general groups:

1. Printed and display material
2. Nonprojected display material
3. Still-projected display material
4. Audio material
5. Linked audio and still-visual material
6. Cine and video materials
7. Computer-mediated materials

When assessing the instructional materials, you should ask yourself what educational objective you want to achieve and what type of sensory experience is required. Teachers are expected to incorporate these materials into their lessons, selecting the most appropriate ones for each specific group of students. Planning lessons to meet the needs of every student is more complicated and time-consuming than ever before.

It is essential that you begin your career with an understanding of the kinds of materials that are available and how they should be used. Your methods courses must expose you to these resources. In fact, your practical classroom experience (known as student teaching, directed teaching, or practicum) should provide opportunities to use a variety of modern resources and materials.

## Technology

Technology is changing all aspects of society, including education. Students today can receive and transmit assignments to their teachers using e-mail. The research capabilities of today's students appear limitless, because the knowledge of the world sits at their fingertips in the form of an Internet connection. For educators, technology promotes teacher creativity that lets you broaden your instruction style.

In Arizona, the Vail School District's "Beyond Textbooks" initiative supplies teachers with digital instruction materials, which keep teachers up-to-date on technology and new ways it can be implemented in the classroom. It also supports teacher collaboration as teachers can share resources over the entire district. Vail's Empire High School, which opened in 2005, uses laptops exclusively in the classroom.

Take a close look at how technology is integrated into the teaching programs you consider. You must be prepared to use this medium in your classroom.

## The Learning Process

Researchers are finding new information about how students learn and process information. Major theories among educators about how students retain information—learning styles, multiple intelligence, and brain-based learning—help teachers better respond to individual students' needs. This means that preparing to teach is more complicated. A teacher can no longer expect to lecture for 40 or 50 minutes, because research suggests that most students do not learn effectively using that method; many students do not have an auditory strength. Learning is viewed as a more active process that requires the teacher to facilitate learning rather than be a source of all knowledge.

Education should reflect the needs of the business world, where individuals are required to work together as a team. Therefore, teachers use team-building strategies such as cooperative learning, which allows students to work together in the learning process while being held responsible for their individual achievement. The theory and methods courses you complete should teach you these methods and allow you to put some of this theory into practice.

## HOW THESE CHANGES AFFECT TEACHER EDUCATION

Teaching sounds complicated, and it is. It is as much an art as it is a science. You must be properly prepared. Teacher education programs are in transition, reflecting the changes taking place in elementary and secondary schools. The factory method of preparing teachers for schools that were bound by the same factory-oriented philosophy of educating children is dying. Because this is a time of transition, some education programs still produce teachers in a traditional manner, whereas other teacher education programs are on the cutting edge. You must find a school that meets the needs of the environment you want to work in. At a minimum, you should be exposed to all of the modern materials, technology, and methods.

## ALTERNATIVE TEACHER EDUCATION PROGRAMS

In the early 1980s, the alternative route to teacher certification began as a way to ward off projected shortages of teachers and replace emergency certification. It has now evolved into a model for recruiting, training, and certifying people who have at least a bachelor's degree and want to become teachers. In 2007, all 50 states and Washington, DC, implemented an alternative route to teacher certification. The term *alternative route* refers to alternatives to the traditional state-approved college-based teacher education program routes for certification. Since its inception, the number of teachers that have earned certification through an alternative route program has risen drastically.

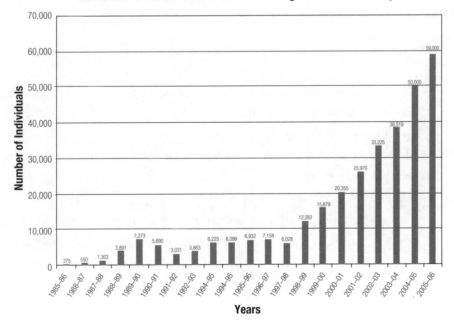

**Individuals Issued Certificates to Teach Through Alternate Routes by Year**

If you already have a bachelor's degree, you may be eligible for alternative teacher certification if the degree is in the subject area to be taught. Generally, state certification boards require individuals to pass approved teacher examinations such as Praxis I and II, complete the professional education courses, and, if appropriate, complete a student teaching requirement. However, states vary in their requirements for alternative teacher education programs; some will allow you to begin teaching right away as long as you enroll in teacher education courses and complete a certain number of courses within a specified time frame.

If you are contemplating changing careers to become a teacher, find out the specific requirements of the state department of education and school district where you want to teach.

## BACHELOR OF SCIENCE DEGREE EDUCATION PROGRAMS

If you are in high school or are a career changer who doesn't hold a bachelor's degree, you will want to investigate bachelor's degree education programs. Finding the right teacher education program can be a challenging task, particularly in this time of educational reform and change. Regardless of your present situation, you should investigate your options carefully. Here are a few questions to consider as you investigate bachelor' degree education programs:

- Can I major in another subject, minor in education, and meet the certification standards of my state?
- Can I have a dual major?
- How many credits are required for my major, and will room remain to take elective courses?
- What are the courses like?
- Can I see a description of the prerequisite, required, and elective courses? Some schools may limit your choices and others may have more variety. The larger schools may offer more options because they have more faculty members to run the courses.

The following sections provide information common to most undergraduate teacher education programs as well as actual program requirements from an exemplary undergraduate teacher education program.

## Mission of the Program

Every teacher education program has a stated mission or overall focus that defines it. The mission of the Harvard Teacher Education Program is specific to teachers wishing to work with students in urban schools: "TEP prepares teachers for the specific challenges of urban education through extensive hands-on training in urban teaching, rigorous coursework, and placements in the center of a vibrant urban environment from day one."

The program's mission will affect every aspect of your educational experience, particularly the curriculum you will study and the kinds of student teaching you can expect.

## Admission Requirements

Admission requirements at colleges and universities vary; however, most teacher education programs have some basic requirements in common. These requirements act as filters to ensure that only the best candidates become teachers. Certain requirements based on your high school career must be met to be accepted by a college or university. Likewise, another set of requirements must be met to be accepted into a teacher education program. How important are these admission requirements? Some schools limit or control the number of students entering the teacher education program. Typically you would apply for admission to the teaching program as a junior, so a large part of what determines whether you will be allowed to enter the teacher education program will be your performance as a college freshman and sophomore. Thus, if you apply to an institution that has enrollment controls, such as Penn State University or the University of Wisconsin–Madison, your academic performance from your first day on campus is extremely important.

Most teacher education programs have the following basic admission requirements:

- minimum coursework in a general degree and/or major area (usually 50–60 hours)
- minimum cumulative grade point average (GPA) in the first two years of college (usually 2.5; however, some programs may require a 3.0 or higher GPA)
- score at or above required levels on a state or national teacher's examination (some candidates also may be required to pass a content area examination)
- core of education courses specified by the certification program (typically, introductory and methods education courses)
- early field experience approved by the teacher education program (for example, tutoring at-risk students or working as a volunteer teacher aide)
- essays and/or interviews (faculties at some colleges evaluate how applicants write and interact with others before granting admission to the degree program)
- reference letters regarding your character and your ability to teach

## KEEP YOUR STANDARDS HIGH

The first two years of college are the most difficult for many students because they must adjust to the rigors of college. Your performance during this period, however, could determine whether or not you gain admission to a teacher education degree program in your junior year.

In some colleges, you must apply for admission to a specific department after successfully completing two years of required courses. Find out whether this policy applies at the school that you are considering. What would happen if your grades did not meet dmission—or are you certain that you can make the grade?

43

e Requirements

have general requirements you must meet before you can
Iowever, like the admission requirements, they vary from

institution to institution. Some of the more common degree requirements you will have to meet to get your teacher education degree are listed here:

- minimum number of credit hours (usually 120 to 130 hours for a bachelor's degree)
- minimum overall GPA in your major and minor fields of study and in your professional education courses
- residency requirement (that is, a certain number of courses or credit hours must be completed at the campus of the school awarding the degree; some schools require that all courses be taken in residence)
- coursework for teacher certification, including education courses
- general studies coursework (sometimes referred to as the liberal arts requirements, or courses of study required of all degree candidates) that provides the foundation for more advanced study
- major and minor courses of study in specific academic areas (which normally require 30+ and 20+ hours, respectively)
- directed teaching or student teaching experience

## MASTER OF ARTS AND MASTER OF SCIENCE DEGREE EDUCATION PROGRAMS

Graduate schools offer one or more of these master's degrees for teachers:

- Master of Arts (MA)
- Master of Education (Ed.M)
- Master of Teaching (MAT)
- Master of Science in Education (MS.Ed.)

Some graduate teacher education programs are meant for people who hold a bachelor's degree with a major outside of teaching—sometimes these programs are called *preservice teacher* programs. That is, the person who is enrolling in the graduate program has little or no teaching experience.

Other graduate teacher education programs focus on the needs of full-time teachers who are obtaining a master's degree to meet permanent st certification requirements. In some states, you need to obtain a degree within a certain number of years after you begin teaching in order to meet the permanent certification requirements of that state. Graduate programs that are geared toward teachers who are already in the field are often called *inservice teacher* programs. Inservice teacher programs may include teachers who do not need to obtain a master's degree to meet certification requirements, but want to further their education for their own professional development or to receive a higher salary. Still other programs include both preservice students and students who are teaching full-time in the same program. This can be an advantage to you if you don't have much teaching experience—you will get to hear opinions, viewpoints, and anecdotes in your classes from teachers who are already in the profession. Programs offered in graduate schools of education include:

- elementary teacher education
- secondary teacher education
- special education
- educational psychology
- curriculum and instruction
- education administration/supervision
- education policy
- student counseling and personnel services

You will find that some graduate programs offer their students more flexibility than others. In fact, some programs enable you to tailor-make your own area of concentration within a general field of education.

Many education departments integrate technology into an educational context. As technology becomes more and more ubiquitous in the classroom setti          mand for such programs is dramatically increasing, as is the grating these concepts and ideas into other, more traditional ms.

master's degree program full-time, you can normally ex- requirements in two semester and two summer sessions. ter's degree programs are shorter and others are longer. of programs, if you start school at the beginning of the he fall and spring semesters, and then the following summer semester, you should be able to graduate from the program by the end of the second summer.

## Master's Degree Admission Requirements

While graduate programs have varying entrance requirements, here are a few basic requirements that are common to most programs:

- bachelor's degree from an accredited college or university
- minimum cumulative GPA in your undergraduate coursework
- for secondary teaching: a certain number of undergraduate or graduate credits in the subject area you are specializing in, or equivalencies, prior to entering the program (usually about 24 credits)
- score at or above required levels on a state or national teachers' examination
- certain minimum scores on the Graduate Record Examination (GRE)
- written personal statement or academic essay
- letters of recommendation regarding your academic skills and/or character

Some programs are much more competitive than others, as you will see once you begin investigating the schools that appeal to you.

You may want to take the GRE before you pick out your desired graduate schools to ensure that you are aiming at the schools where you have a strong chance for being admitted.

## Master's Degree General Requirements

Most universities have general degree requirements. However, like the admissions requirements, they often vary from institution to institution. Here are some of the more common requirements you will have to meet before being awarded your master's degree:

- minimum number of credit hours (can range from less than 30 to over 60, but most programs require around 32 hours)

- minimum overall GPA in your graduate coursework (often, a 3.0 GPA is required)
- special project, thesis, research report, teaching portfolio, or other written work
- student teaching experience
- comprehensive written and/or oral examinations
- complete all requirements for graduation within a specified time frame (usually five to seven years)

## TEACHING SKILLS FOR THE FUTURE

Whether you pursue a graduate or undergraduate teacher education program, the main thing you expect your program to do is prepare you to succeed as a teacher. The criteria listed below, from the American Association of School Personnel Administrators (AASPA) publication *Teacher of the Future: A Continuous Cycle of Improvement*, will help you evaluate teacher education programs, whether they are graduate or undergraduate. AASPA identifies the critical knowledge and skill levels a teacher will need to be successful today and in the future. Look for a teacher education program that promises to provide them.

### Knowledge

In addition to knowing the subjects you teach and how those subjects are related to other subjects, you should know how to:

- teach your subjects to students
- assess student progress on a regular basis
- plan lessons in a logical sequence
- reflect on your own teaching and devise ongoing improvement
- collaborate with educators to create a complete educational environment

- use technology, at least at an intermediate level
- appreciate various cultures and establish rapport with a diverse population
- get information and educate students to seek and evaluate information

## Skills

Besides the knowledge that teachers are required to have, they also should be able to:

- recognize and respond to individual differences in students
- implement a variety of teaching methods that result in higher student achievement
- work cooperatively with parents, colleagues, and others
- display a genuine love of teaching
- implement full-inclusion techniques for special education students
- differentiate instruction for development and ability levels
- write, speak, and present information well
- help students develop critical thinking skills
- relate well to parents and community members
- apply technology
- implement conflict resolution strategies

## Quality Field Education

To gain the knowledge and develop the skills you need, choose a teacher education program that is field-based. In other words, it should offer many opportunities to practice with children in actual classroom settings throughout the program—not only in your student teaching experience. The theory of teaching is important; however, the practice is crucial in preparing you to meet the challenges you will face in your future classrooms.

## GETTING THE MOST FROM STUDENT TEACHING

The best preparation for the classroom is *experience in the classroom*. Your student teaching, directed teaching, or field experience is the crucial component before taking over your own classroom. Teacher training is an ongoing process, and experienced teachers will tell you they continue to learn new methods and technology (especially technology) every year. But you must begin somewhere, and that first experience—student teaching—is vitally important.

To have a successful student teaching experience, you should keep several points in mind:

- Establish a good rapport with all those around you, including your cooperating teacher, other teachers, your students, the principal, and support staff.
- Do not be afraid to ask for help.
- Take criticism as it is given—constructively.
- Be prompt, conscientious, and tactful.
- Be willing to do more than is asked of you.
- Accept that you cannot totally be your own person or do your own thing.
- Remember, it is not your classroom. The professional and legal obligation for what happens still rests with the cooperating teacher.
- Make a concerted effort to learn to plan, organize, and manage.
- Do not be afraid to use some of the materials and activities of your cooperating teacher, but develop and use some of your own, too.
- Although it may sometimes feel as if your primary objective is to "just survive," remember that student teaching is designed to allow you to grow and develop as a teacher.
- Do not be consumed by the deadlines, pressures, and rigors of student teaching— try to find ways to get away from it (both literally and figuratively). You will need to start fresh and renewed every day and every week.

## MEETING STATE CERTIFICATION REQUIREMENTS

In most cases, you are not automatically certified as a teacher upon graduation from an accredited teacher education program. You must file an application for a license (certification) with the state department of education in the state where you will be working and meet all of their requirements.

Every state requires a bachelor's degree, but requirements that vary include the kinds of courses taken and the exams that are required. The course of study in most teacher education programs matches the exact requirements for teacher certification *in that state*. However, if you plan to teach in another state, you may have to add a course or specialized requirement to your studies. It is worthwhile to choose a teacher education program in the state where you ultimately want to teach—or at least to know the certification requirements for that state when you start school—so you can fulfill them as you study. See Chapter 4 for a list of state departments of education and contact the ones where you may want to teach or study to request information about specific requirements. Chapter 4 also lists the basic certification requirements for each state along with contact information for all of the state certification boards.

## CHOOSING YOUR PROGRAM

When you consider different programs, reflect on the kind of environment that suits your personality, budget, and family needs. Evaluate each factor separately, first, and then put them together. There may be numerous schools for you to consider, or you may be limited by circumstances such as commuting distance, cost of the program, and personal situation. If possible, apply to several different colleges or universities because there is no guarantee of gaining admission to the college of your choice.

Applying to a college can be a lengthy process that costs both time and money. For each application—which may be quite lengthy—you must write an essay, pay an application fee, enclose letters of recommendation and copies of transcripts, and take and sometimes achieve a certain score on one or more entrance exams.

Before you send in any applications, however, check to see that the college or university you are planning to attend has an *accredited* teacher education program. A mishmash of courses taken at different colleges may not meet the requirements necessary for state certification. Most states require the school you attend to sign off on your credentials and grades.

## What to Look For in a Program

Selecting a teacher education program that matches your personality and career goals is critical to your success as a teacher. A good teacher education program should:

- offer courses that ensure your preparation to teach in your chosen field or specialization
- have admission criteria that examine your personality traits
- require practicum experiences connected with your college coursework
- provide opportunities for you to work in community schools as a teacher's aide
- offer a broad range of courses that allow you to study teaching and learning theories that have been validated by examined practice, research, and conventional wisdom
- provide opportunities through coursework, seminars, observations, and interviews for you to examine and reflect on your beliefs and values about teaching and schooling
- provide opportunities for you to become inducted into the teaching profession by offering a variety of organizations for students in the program
- recognize that there is not one best way to teach and that your teaching style will be a function of many things, including your personality traits, beliefs, and learning style
- provide a variety of feedback mechanisms that serve as markers to measure your growth as a teacher
- avoid "baptism by fire" approaches that induct you into the rigors of teaching before you are ready
- avoid "ivory tower" approaches that totally isolate you from the real life of classrooms and the joys of teaching

## Focus on Academic Quality

There are many factors to consider in selecting a school, but the quality of professional training it provides must be your primary concern. First, make sure that the school's teacher education program is accredited. Then, look for the specific concentrations or specializations you are interested in—the right academic fit. Finally, evaluate the overall quality of the program.

## Accreditation

Each state department of education allows you to take the certification exams and apply for a provisional license immediately on graduation from an accredited program. A school that is accredited has been positively evaluated based on the essential courses needed to prepare teachers to begin their careers. Ensure that the accreditation is specifically for the undergraduate or graduate department you are planning to apply to.

### RED FLAGS WHEN CHOOSING A TEACHER EDUCATION PROGRAM

There are more than 300 unaccredited universities operating in the United States and about 200 fake accrediting agencies. When investigating teacher education programs, lookout for these warning signs:

- addresses that are suites or PO box numbers
- names that are similar to well-known colleges or universities
- degrees that can be earned in less time than at a traditional college
- programs that give credits for lifetime or real-world experience
- little or no interaction with professors and/or advisors
- tuition that is paid per degree rather than per credit

For undergraduate degrees, if you want to major in a curriculum such as psychology or political science *and* want to teach, find out whether you can have a dual major or whether you can minor in education and still meet the requirements for certification. If not, you can meet all of your education requirements in a graduate teacher education degree program and have the benefit of studying another area as an undergraduate. Some states are changing their certification requirements, expecting teachers to have a curriculum concentration in addition to teaching methods coursework.

## IS THIS A QUALITY PROGRAM?

There are many ways of evaluating the quality of a teacher education program besides its accreditation. Several questions can help you determine the quality of a program. Each consideration will vary in importance from person to person, and of course the best quality elementary education program in the world will do you no good if you want to specialize in high school math. Consider the quality of the program when choosing your school—it could make the difference between success and failure in your first year of teaching.

- **Can I sit in on a course?** It is important to see how small or large the classes are and how they are conducted.

- **Can I speak to someone in the program?** Speaking with a current student gives you the inside scoop about life in that college and will help you determine whether you will feel comfortable in that environment.

- **What methodology does the program promote: traditional, experience-based, or both?** It is *essential* that you leave college with a variety of methods to use in the classroom. Students learn in very different ways, and you must understand which teaching techniques work best with each learning style. If the college you are considering does not have a hands-on approach to instruction, they probably have not updated their curriculum. You should be able to use and understand cooperative learning, whole language, theories of multiple intelligences, the discovery or museum approach, process writing, portfolio assessment, and all other kinds of interactive methodology *in addition to* direct traditional instruction.

- **Is the career planning and placement office helpful?** The career counselors should be able to help you secure a job after graduation.

- **What is the attrition rate in the program?** Students who start the program should be able to finish it. The higher the percentage of students who stay, the stronger the department.

- **What kind of fieldwork will I do?** The college should place you in a school early in the program. Experience as a student observer, student participant, or student teacher may help you decide what level or what area you want to specialize in. Doing fieldwork strongly reinforces your credentials, and the more experience you have, the more attractive a candidate you will be to potential employers.

- **Will I be prepared to take the certification exams?** Many states allow you to begin teaching before you complete the licensing exams. Eventually, however, you must take them. Although the exams vary from state to state, the school should help you with the certification process.

## Nonacademic Concerns

Once you have a sense of what you want from your teacher education program, consider nonacademic concerns. These concerns apply to all prospective students.

## Admissions Standards

Take a realistic look at your grades and other credentials. What kind of student are you? Admission standards vary, and colleges are classified by their degree of competitiveness and the relative importance of grades on your application. Top-ranked schools attract students with the highest grades and strongest academic portfolios. Other schools have easier admission policies, which means that your chances of being admitted are better. Select one school you would ideally like to attend (sometimes called your "reach") and some schools that are less competitive (often referred to as "safe" because they have less strict admission standards).

## Cost of Tuition and Fees

There was a time that a higher education was very inexpensive, but those days seem to be gone for good in the United States. You are literally shopping for a school, and it should fit both your pocketbook and your resources.

Every state has a system of state colleges and universities. Generally, tuition is considerably lower at a state college or university than at a private one. Residents of a given state normally pay less tuition to attend an in-state college or university than students from other states. In fact, the total non-resident fees are often comparable to private school tuition. Some states are more generous than others to out-of-state students, so investigate all costs carefully.

## Public or Private?

One of the ways public universities keep costs down is by holding large classes. Courses during the first few years are often given in large lecture halls and are attended by hundreds of students at the same time. Occasionally, a course is given at one location and broadcast by satellite to other schools. Can you learn under these circumstances? Private schools also have some large lecture classes and satellite broadcasts, but such programs are usually kept to a minimum.

Private universities may be geared to a specific population. Some are supported by a religious organization, and the values and culture of that belief system may permeate the entire environment. It can be very comforting to know you have a shared experience, prior to college, with your new friends and classmates. At a small school, you may feel uncomfortable if you are not part of the religious majority. However, many fine colleges run by religious organizations attract a large population of students who do not adhere to that religion; thus, it would be difficult to identify that school's religious affiliation by talking to students or sitting in on classes.

## Size and Culture

Colleges come in all sizes, and the size of the college or university you choose can have a major effect on your comfort and happiness. If you grew up in a small town or city, you may think a small rural college is the place for you. Such schools offer a secure environment, where everyone eventually gets to know each other; they may even enroll as few as several hundred students. Often, small schools have a limited variety of courses. There may be a very homogeneous student population.

On the other hand, you may be looking for a school that has a large and diverse student body, a busy social atmosphere, various athletic programs, and opportunities to meet people from many different backgrounds. A university usually has many colleges (e.g., liberal arts, engineering, sciences) on its campus as well as several graduate programs. Both part-time and full-time students attend classes; some students live on campus, and others commute. Because people are constantly coming and going, you can be more anonymous on a large campus. It is possible to feel a bit isolated, but you can make friends with students who have similar interests.

Make an effort to find the right-sized school, because being happy will enhance your college experience. Ask yourself, *What kind of student life do I want?* A small rural school might eventually bore you, or a large university with the great football team might be overwhelming.

## Location Matters

Schools are located in every part of the country, and your ability to find true happiness may depend on where you settle for the years it will take to complete your program.

Small rural and suburban colleges and universities are often enclosed units. There may literally be a wall surrounding the entire campus, providing a feeling of security. All of the buildings are located on the grounds, including classrooms, dormitories, dining halls, recreation centers, and the library.

In contrast, a college or university in a large city usually encompasses many city blocks. Although the buildings are within a given area, the streets are open to pedestrian and vehicular traffic. Business establishments, bookstores, dormitories, art galleries, food stores, restaurants, banks, clothing stores, museums, and movie theaters may be mixed in with the classroom buildings. It can be a very exciting environment for one person but very difficult for another person to adjust to.

## Climate Control

If you live in Florida or Tennessee, can you adjust to the cold weather of Maine or Michigan? There are excellent schools all over the northern United States, but winter brings cold and snow—and the difficulties associated with such a climate. The University of Wisconsin–Madison, for example, is an excellent university with a wonderful education program and a beautiful campus, but winter temperatures can drop to minus 40. That's forty degrees *below zero*!

People who live in temperate climates often love the change of seasons. Attending school in southern Florida or California will provide opportunities for sun and fun, but can you live with one season year-round?

## The Distance Factor

If you are a working adult with a family of your own, you may not have much of a choice in the location of your school if your spouse needs to be near work and your children want to stay in their schools.

If you are single, how far away from your parents and friends do you really want to be? Many students initially think that the distance away from home doesn't matter, only to find that it does. No matter how involved you are on campus, there always comes a point when you will want to go home, or family and friends will want to visit you.

One consideration in distance is whether you can make the trip back and forth in one day. Costs increase if your parents have to stay in a motel when they come to visit. If you are invited home for a special occasion, could you do it in time to be back for classes? If the school is close enough to drive to in a short period of time, you will be able to come and go more easily.

If you are considering going further away, is the plane ride an easy one? Do you have to make many connections, or can you do it without great complications? How much is the plane fare? If the school is so far from your home that you cannot travel, be aware that you may be shut out of your dorm during some breaks.

## Housing Options

Many colleges and universities that have dorms insist that freshmen live on campus because it helps them form a community of friends who will become a support system. Some schools have wonderful educational programs but no dormitories; therefore, you must rent a room or an apartment on your own. This can be difficult to do as a freshman if you don't know many people. Many colleges have special apartments available for married students with or without children, either on campus or in a nearby community.

### TAKE A TRIP

You really must visit a campus before you accept an offer of admission, because a mismatch can affect your happiness, your grades, and, ultimately, your future career.

Many colleges give guided tours for prospective students and their families during the application period. Most have a counselor available to speak to you about the coursework and other concerns. Some colleges even have special weekends during which prospective students can spend time in the dorms with students who have similar interests and career aspirations.

## DISTANCE LEARNING TEACHER EDUCATION PROGRAMS

If, after reading all about traditional education programs, it just doesn't seem feasible for you to physically attend classes on a campus, you can opt for a distance learning teacher education program. These days, it's possible to earn an entire undergraduate or graduate degree by participating in a distance learning program. This means you learn the same material as you would by participating in traditional classes; however, your education is done at home, at your own pace, through reading, participating in online courses, and taking exams.

Depending on the course of study, students may not need to be enrolled full-time, and they usually have more flexible schedules for finishing their work. Taking courses by distance study is often more challenging and time-consuming than attending classes, however, especially for adults who have other obligations. Success depends on an individual student's motivation. Students usually do reading assignments on their own. Written exercises, which they complete and send to an instructor for grading, supplement their reading material.

Assuming you pass the exams associated with the distance learning program, the end result and the degree or certification you earn is identical to what someone who attended a traditional educational institution would earn.

Distance learning programs may or may not have a residency requirement; therefore, be sure to investigate carefully each program you are considering. Some schools offer only one or more education courses via distance learning, while others offer entire degrees.

For more information on distance learning, go to the United States Distance Learning Association's website at http://www.usdla.org/.

## MAKING YOUR CHOICE

There are hundreds of teacher education programs with unique classes and stringent requirements. Do not look for easy; look for useful. Look for a program that will turn you into a good teacher—knowledgeable and reflective of the needs of your community and world.

It may seem an insurmountable task to become certified as a teacher. But it's not; thousands of people have become teachers, and you can, too. One key is to plan, early and carefully. Another is to have good information. Then, make your decisions one at a time.

Do your homework. Get as much information as possible *now*, so your college experience will be a great beginning to a wonderful career!

### THE INSIDE TRACK

| | |
|---|---|
| Who: | Tracey Loller |
| What: | First Grade |
| Where: | Donegan Elementary, Bethlehem, PA |
| Type of School: | Title I (90% of students are on free/reduced lunch; therefore, we receive additional educational funding for support teachers and interventions) |
| How long: | Seven years |
| How much: | $48,000 |
| Degree(s): | BS Elem/Early Childhood, M.Ed. Reading Specialist, English as a Second Language Certification |
| School(s): | BS Millersville University, M.Ed. Kutztown University, ESOL |
| Certification: | DeSales University |

### Insider Advice

I would advise anyone interested in teaching to gain as much experience as possible working with students in the age group you wish to teach. I would also suggest putting a great deal of effort into your student teaching experience.

It can help you to obtain a good recommendation. You should also use this opportunity to visit other teachers and experience the different ways that teachers accomplish so much. What works for one teacher may not work for another. This also applies to individual students. Be prepared, your first year can be very overwhelming.

### What I Wish I Had Learned in School

More on how to reach the student who is unmotivated to learn. More on how to create positive working relationships with parents. More on using positive reinforcement and reward systems to promote good behavior, without spending a lot of money on material rewards.

### Greatest Joys

When students from the past come back to visit me, I really feel like I touched their lives. Also, every time a struggling learner masters a task, and when I hear students encouraging each other to succeed.

### Biggest Drawback

Dealing with uncooperative parents, who just don't seem to see what is most important for their children due to troubles within their own lives. Constantly adapting to an ever-changing curriculum that is based on state testing results.

### Future Plans

To remain working with students from low-income areas, many of whom really need to have good role models in their lives.

# CHAPTER three

## FINDING FINANCIAL AID

**A COLLEGE** education is a major expense and college prices are rising. The average private four-year college tuition was $25,143 from 2008 to 2009—up 5.9% from the previous year. In 2008–2009, the average public four-year tuition was $6,585 (up 6.4% from the previous year). And for public two-year tuition, students paid an average of $2,402 (up 4.7% from the previous year). While these figures can seem frightening, according to a 2007 College Board Study the gap in earning potential between a high school diploma and a BA over a lifetime is more than $800,000. So, think of your education as an investment in yourself.

This chapter gives you the tools you need to find financial aid to help you finance that education. Once you find the best teacher education program for you, the next step is to determine how to pay for it. You can use financial aid and scholarships to help you save hundreds and even thousands of dollars over the course of your education program. You'll find out how to determine your eligibility for financial aid, and where you can get specific loans, grants, and scholarships.

## FINANCIAL AID FOR THE EDUCATION YOU NEED

There are many different types of financial aid available, plus an even larger selection of scholarships for which you may be eligible. Chances are, you can qualify even if you're attending only part-time. The financial aid you'll get may be less than that for longer, full-time programs, but it still can help you pay for a portion of your teacher education program. Also, if you're currently employed, be sure to contact your employer to determine if it will cover any part of your education. Even if you can't get tuition assistance for all your required courses, perhaps you can at least take some electives or general education classes under an employer-based tuition assistance or reimbursement plan.

Most people's first reaction to hearing the cost of college tuition is, "I can't afford this!" Remember that there are many ways to finance your education; you *do not* have to write a check for the full amount at the outset. Few students and their families have the resources to pay the cost of four years of college. Many find it necessary to acquire money from a variety of sources. Determining your financial need is a crucial first step in preparing to go to college.

Financial aid officers at colleges work with a formula that is consistent nationwide. They evaluate your income, assets, and debts and come up with an amount that they believe you can afford. Using this dollar amount, they build a financial aid package that will supplement your assets.

## GETTING STARTED

The first step in the financial aid process is to get a form that is called *Free Application for Federal Student Aid* (FAFSA). You need to get this form, fill it out, and file it because it is the foundation of so many different types of financial aid. In fact, most schools will not process your request for loans, work-study programs, or any other financial assistance until you file this form. Because the FAFSA, as it is commonly referred to, is such an integral part of the financial aid process, it is the best place to start.

You can get this important form online at http://www.fafsa.ed.gov/. (It is included in Appendix C to help you become familiar with its components.) You will request a PIN, which allows you to complete the entire process on-line, without having to print any signature forms. Otherwise, you can print out, sign, and send in the signature pages.

Approximately 15 million students use the Free Application for Federal Student Aid each year. According to the federal government, anyone in the process of applying to school should complete the FAFSA form. "Many families mistakenly think they don't qualify for aid and prevent themselves from receiving financial aid by failing to apply for it. In addition, there are a few sources of aid, such as unsubsidized Stafford and PLUS Loans, that are available regardless of need. The FAFSA form is free. There is no good excuse for not applying," explains one FAFSA brochure.

The Federal Student Aid Information Center can help you complete the application and provides the public with free information. Call 1-800-4-FED-AID to speak to a specialist.

## ARE YOU CONSIDERED DEPENDENT OR INDEPENDENT?

When you apply for financial aid, your answers to certain questions will determine whether you're considered dependent on your parents and must report their income and assets as well as your own, or whether you're independent and must report only your own income and assets (and those of your spouse if you're married).

If you are a dependent student, you will need financial information from your parents in order to complete the FAFSA. Read the following list to determine if you are dependent or independent according to financial aid rules. You are considered an independent student if you meet any one of the following criteria:

- You are at least 24 years old.
- You are married.

- You have a dependent other than a spouse.
- You are a graduate student or professional student.
- You are a ward of the court or an orphan.
- You are a veteran of the U.S. Armed Forces.

The need analysis service or federal processor looks at the following if you are a dependent student:

- family assets, including savings, stocks and bonds, real estate investments, business/farm ownership, and trusts
- parents' age and need for retirement income
- number of children and other dependents in the family household
- number of family members in college
- cost of attendance, also called student expense budget, including tuition/fees, books and supplies, room and board (living with parents, on campus or off campus), transportation, and personal expenses

## HELP FROM THE PROS

Every year, in many high schools across the country, guidance and career counselors hold one- or two-night workshops on financial aid for students and parents. Some community colleges offer a similar service. Once you have some of the basic information, counselors will advise you to contact the financial aid office of a local college or university to discuss loans and scholarships.

## GATHERING YOUR RECORDS

To complete the FAFSA, you'll need to gather the following:

- Records for income earned in the year prior to when you will start school. (You may also need records of your parent or parents' income information.) For the 2009–2010 school year, you will need 2008 information.
- Your Social Security card and driver's license
- W-2 Forms or other records of income earned
- Your (and your spouse's, if you are married) federal income tax return
- Your parent's federal income tax return if you are considered dependent

- Records of any untaxed income received such as welfare benefits, social security benefits, Temporary Assistance for Needy Families (TANF), veteran's benefits, or military or clergy allowances
- Current bank statements and records of stocks, bonds, and other investments
- Business or farm records, if applicable
- Your alien registration card (if you are not a U.S. citizen)

## DETERMINING YOUR ELIGIBILITY

To receive financial aid from an accredited college or institution's student aid program, you must be a U.S. citizen or an eligible non-citizen with a Social Security number. Check with Immigration and Naturalization Service (INS) if you are not a U.S. citizen and are unsure of your eligibility (call 800-375-5283 or visit http://www.ins.usdoj.gov/graphics/index.htm).

Eligibility is a very complicated matter, but it can be simplified to the following two equations.

Your contribution + Your parents' contribution
= Expected family contribution

Cost of attendance – Expected family contribution = Your financial need

## AVOID COMMON MISTAKES

To maximize your chances of receiving the best possible financial aid package, you have to not only file the FAFSA application *on time* but also *do it right*. Information that is incorrect or incomplete may result in your application being rejected! To avoid mistakes, read the instructions carefully, take your time, be honest, double-check your work, and ask someone else to check it, too. Some common errors include:

- omitting untaxed income information (student or parents)
- omitting Title IV income exclusion amounts (students commonly don't report their work-study earnings, and parents tend to omit the amount of child support they pay)

- forgetting to sign the application, which causes the application to be rejected
- reporting assets valued at a lower amount than the asset debt on the student and parent asset section of the application (if the asset debt is listed as being greater than the asset value, the application will be rejected)
- filing the FAFSA under the student's nickname or a shortened version of their legal name (the name on the application must match records at the Social Security Administration, Immigration and Naturalization Service, and/or Selective Service)

## TYPES OF FINANCIAL AID

Many kinds of financial aid are available from the federal government. Other sources of financial aid include your state, the college or university, foundations and other nonprofit groups, and private organizations and benefactors. You can find out about many kinds of financial aid through your local high school or library or through the financial aid office of your college or university.

### Federal Grants

Federal grants *do not* have to be paid back to the federal government. A Pell Grant is one example; every student who qualifies for a Pell Grant is guaranteed funding. Another example is a Federal Supplemental Educational Opportunity Grant (FSEOG), which is awarded to students with the lowest expected family contributions; however, FSEOGs are not guaranteed, so not every eligible student will receive an award.

In some cases, you may receive a Pell Grant for attending a post baccalaureate teacher certificate program. In 2008, $16,428,110,000 was available through the Pell Grant, resulting in grants ranging from $400 to $4,731.

FSEOGs are *campus-based programs*. In government parlance, a campus-based program is simply one that is administered by the financial aid office of a college or university (as opposed to a grant or loan administered by a federal or other agency). Not every school participates in campus-based programs, but most do. For FSEOG, priority is given to those with "exceptional need" and those who are also Pell Grant recipients. Visit www.ed.gov/programs for additional information.

## Federal Loans

There are many loans available to students—a few are discussed here.

### Perkins Loans

Awarded to students with exceptional financial need, these loans carry a very low interest rate. The Perkins Loan Program is a campus-based program. The loan is made directly to the school.

Depending on when you apply, your level of need, and the funding level of the school, you can borrow up to $4,000 for each year of undergraduate study for up to five years. Graduate students can borrow up to $6,000 per year.

The school pays you directly by check or credits your tuition account. You have a specified period of time after you graduate (provided you were continuously enrolled at least half-time) to begin repayment.

### REQUIREMENTS FOR FEDERAL FINANCIAL AID

To qualify for federal student aid, you must meet certain requirements:

- be a U.S. citizen or an eligible non-citizen
- be registered with the Selective Service (if required)
- attend a college that participates in federal financial aid programs
- work toward a degree or certificate
- make satisfactory academic progress
- not owe a refund on a federal grant or be in default on a federal educational loan
- have financial need as determined by the FAFSA

In addition, you may be considered *ineligible* for federal financial aid if you ever have been convicted of drug distribution or possession.

### William D. Ford Direct and Federal Family Education Stafford Loans (FFEL)

These loans are the major source of financial aid for students. Whereas the application processes for the two loans are similar, the financial aid is distributed differently. The Ford Direct Loan is borrowed directly from the federal government, and the loan is processed through the school. FFEL Stafford Loans are processed through a lender such as a bank.

### Parent Loan for Undergraduate Students (PLUS) Loans

These loans enable parents with good credit histories to borrow money to pay education expenses of a child who is a dependent undergraduate student enrolled at least half-time. To be eligible, your parents must meet citizenship requirements and pass a credit check. If they don't pass the credit check, they might still be able to receive a loan if they can show that extenuating circumstances exist or if someone who is able to pass the credit check agrees to cosign the loan.

The annual limit on a PLUS Loan is equal to your cost of attendance minus any other financial aid you receive. For instance, if your cost of attendance is $6,000 and you receive $4,000 in other financial aid, your parents could borrow up to, but no more than, $2,000. The interest rate varies, but as of July 1, 2006, the interest rate for PLUS Loans was 8.5%. Your parents must begin repayment while you're still in school—there is no grace period. For more information, go to http://www.parentplusloan.com/plus-loans/.

## THE VOCABULARY OF FORD DIRECT AND FFEL STAFFORD LOANS

Ford Direct and FFEL Stafford Loans can be subsidized or unsubsidized. An *unsubsidized* loan is not based on need, and you will be charged interest from the time the loan is disbursed until it is repaid. A *subsidized* loan is awarded on the basis of need, and you will not be charged any interest until repayment begins; the federal government pays the interest while you are enrolled in college. A *deferment* allows you to postpone repayment until you graduate. Usually, repayment for either of these loans begins six months after you graduate. By that time you probably will be employed, earning an income that allows you to repay the loan.

The interest rate is generally lower for these loans than for other kinds of loans, but *interest continues to be added*, or capitalized, to an unsubsidized loan while you are enrolled in school. Capitalization increases the total amount of the loan to be repaid.

## Special Loan Programs for Teachers

As you investigate loan options for your teacher education program, be on the lookout for special loan forgiveness programs for teachers.

Some states currently offer some form of a loan forgiveness program for students who will make a commitment to teach in that state for a certain number of years. In some states, you are eligible for the loan forgiveness program only if you are planning to enter a critical shortage area, such as special education, math, or science. Contact your state department of education for details.

The Federal Teacher Loan Forgiveness Program is directed for those who teach full-time for five consecutive complete academic years in certain elementary and secondary schools that serve low-income families and meet other qualifications. These teachers may be eligible for forgiveness of up to $5,000, and in some cases up to $17,500. To apply, download the Teacher Loan Forgiveness Application at http://www.aessuccess .org/manage/cant_make_payment/Federal_Teacher_Loan_Forgiveness .shtml and mail it to:

AES/PHEAA
Attn: Loan Discharge
1200 N. 7th Street
Harrisburg, PA 17102-1444

## Work-Study Programs

A variety of work-study programs are available as a form of financial aid. If you already know what school you want to attend, you can find out about its school-based work-study options from the student employment office. Job possibilities may include on- or off-campus jobs. Another type of work-study program is called the Federal Work-Study (FWS) program, and it can be applied for on the FAFSA.

The federal work-study program provides jobs for undergraduate and graduate students *with financial need* allowing them to earn money to help pay education expenses. The program encourages community service work and provides hands-on experience related to a student's course of study, when available. The amount of the FWS award depends on:

- when you apply (the earlier you apply, the better)
- your level of financial need
- the funds that are available at your particular school

Your FWS salary will be at least the current federal minimum wage or higher depending on the type of work you do and the skills required. As an undergraduate, you'll be paid by the hour (a graduate student may receive a salary), and you will receive the money directly from your school at least monthly. The awards are not transferable from year to year. Not all schools participate in the FWS program.

You will be assigned a job on campus, in a private nonprofit organization, or in a public agency that offers a public service. The total hourly wages you earn in each year cannot exceed your total FWS award for that year, and you cannot work more than 20 hours per week.

## Private Financial Aid

Other forms of financial aid are available in the form of grants and scholarships that are not funded by the federal government. The school you are applying to may offer you scholarships and loans based on available funds; these amounts vary greatly from one school to the next. Wealthier schools (with large endowments) may offer loans at a low interest rate—or even scholarship money, which does not have to be paid back—as part of your financial aid package. And there are many other sources of money besides your own school.

### Grants

Grants may be based on merit or need. A student may receive a grant to research a topic in a specific subject area or because of a combination of interest in a particular subject area and financial need. The federal government, businesses, and private organizations fund most grants, which usually do not have to be repaid. However, if you receive a research-related grant, you will have to keep careful records of your research activities to satisfy the grant administrators.

## Scholarships

Scholarships come in a variety of packages and probably require the most effort on your part to obtain. You will hear and read about many scholarship opportunities, to the point that you think everyone is paying their college tuition through a scholarship. The reality of the situation is, *most of the scholarship dollars are awarded to the top 5% of graduating seniors in a given year.* However, if you are willing to spend some time searching for scholarships that meet your talents, the rewards can be surprising.

*Kinds and Sources.* There are many sources of scholarships including:

- local, state, and federal government
- colleges and universities
- U.S. military
- businesses and companies
- individuals or families
- organizations and clubs

Scholarships are offered on the basis of merit, usually in academics, athletics, or the arts. A student may receive partial or full tuition, and a scholarship may be renewable (annually) or nonrenewable (a one-time award). Scholarships do not have to be repaid, but the recipient has to meet certain application criteria (as determined by the awarding source) as well as certain standards of performance if the scholarship is to be renewed.

*Where They Are.* To begin, visit your school counselor or the financial aid office of a local college. Your local library also may be a rich source of scholarship information. Many universities have web sites that allow you to conduct online scholarship searches. A scholarship search allows you to type in a few descriptors (your interests and talents), which are matched to available scholarships. Then, it is up to you to request, complete, and submit the application before the deadline.

You can search online for scholarships by visiting www.fastweb.com and www.collegenet.com.

At **www.fastweb.com**, if you answer a series of questions about yourself and your education interests and goals, you will receive a list of scholarships for which you may qualify. Their database is updated regularly, and your list will be updated when new scholarships are added that fit your profile.

At **www.collegenet.com**, you can search a database of scholarship awards and also narrow your search by entering your gender, age, and major.

Some applications are short, and others are extremely detailed—be prepared to work for the money! Keep in mind that most scholarships are very competitive, and you should apply only for those for which you are truly qualified. It would be to your advantage to have your counselor read and comment on each application before you submit it.

*Unexpected Sources.* Scholarships are sometimes awarded after you have been in a particular department and proven your academic abilities. Once you enter the college of your choice, contact the head of the teacher education department to find out about scholarships for prospective teachers. Knowing the criteria for a particular scholarship, you can *plan* to compete for it. We said it was hard work!

If you're currently employed, check to see if your employer has scholarship funds or tuition reimbursement programs available. If you're a dependent student, ask your parents and aunts, uncles, and cousins to check with their employers or organizations they belong to for possible aid sources. You never know what type of scholarships you might dig up. For example, any of the following groups may know of money that could be yours:

- professional teacher associations
- religious organizations
- fraternal organizations
- clubs, such as the Boy Scouts and Girl Scouts, Rotary, Kiwanis, American Legion, or 4H
- athletic clubs
- veterans groups
- ethnic group associations
- unions

Some school districts are desperate to hire candidates in certain areas. The New York City school system has a scholarship program called Teach New York. Because of the great need for bilingual general special education teachers and bilingual and monolingual teachers for several subspecialties of special education—hearing impaired, visually impaired, and speech impaired—students can receive paid graduate or undergraduate tuition (depending on the program) in return for several years of paid teaching service. These are wonderful opportunities for a student! The key to finding them is being a good detective.

Phi Delta Kappa is an international association of professional educators that offers national teacher scholarships. To obtain more information about the organization and the scholarships it offers, contact them at:

Scholarship Programs
Phi Delta Kappa International
P.O. Box 789
Bloomington, IN 47402-0789
scholarships@pdkintl.org
www.pdkintl.org

*Be Realistic.* Most scholarships have very definite eligibility requirements such as GPA, attendance, and participation in school activities and organizations. Although no one should tell you not to apply for a particular scholarship, you should *direct your efforts toward the scholarships that best match your qualifications.*

If you are going into teaching from another career—especially if you already hold a bachelor's degree—obtaining grants and scholarships may be difficult. This should not discourage you from applying, but you'll probably have better results if you focus on grants and scholarships that are based on research or academic performance.

As you look for sources of scholarships, continue to enhance your chances of winning one by participating in extracurricular events and volunteer activities. You should also obtain letters of reference from people who know you well and are leaders in the community, so you can submit their names or letters of recommendation with your scholarship applications.

Make a list of any awards you've received or other special honors that you could list on your scholarship application.

### A WORD OF CAUTION

Many reputable companies will help you do a scholarship search, for a fee. In most cases, these companies access the same information that you, too, can access with a little effort. First try searching yourself, with the help of a school counselor. If that search does not satisfy your needs, only then consider paying for professional services.

## WHEN TO APPLY FOR FINANCIAL AID

Applying to college and obtaining financial aid requires planning. If you are changing your career, apply for financial aid as soon as you know which semester you will enroll. If you are in high school, begin the process during your sophomore year. Attend college days or fairs during your sophomore year to start getting an idea which colleges and universities are located in your local area or state.

Recruiters attend college fairs to distribute information about their colleges and universities. You can learn about schools that you might wish to visit in the future, and the kinds and amount of financial aid that each college offers. Some colleges participate in certain federal programs and not in others; it is a good idea to find out this information early on.

Colleges and universities are continually improving their financial aid services to increase the opportunities for more students to attend their institutions. Check with the financial aid office of the college or university you think you will attend to keep abreast of any changes in the financial aid program. Continue to check with the financial aid office about any changes after you start school.

### A WORD TO THE WISE

Most of the financial aid that you will receive will be in the form of loans. Some of these loans will allow you to borrow more than you need. Remember: At some time or another, you will have to repay these loans. Before you borrow, consider your future income. Don't borrow more than you can realistically project that you will be able to afford to repay. This is your responsibility to yourself and to students who will need this money in the future.

## MAXIMIZE YOUR ELIGIBILITY FOR LOANS AND SCHOLARSHIPS

Loans and scholarships are often awarded based on your eligibility. Depending on the type of loan or scholarship you pursue, the eligibility requirements will be different.

Pay off your consumer debt, such as credit card and auto loan balances. Minimize your capital gains.

Improve your eligibility when applying for loans and/or scholarships by saving money in your parent's name, rather than in your name. Ask family members to wait until you graduate before giving money to help with education.

If parents are considering going back to school, they should do so at the same time as their children. The more family members in school simultaneously, the more aid will be available to each.

If you believe that your family's financial circumstances are unusual, make an appointment with the financial aid administrator at your school to review your case. Sometimes the school will be able to adjust your financial aid package to compensate.

### THE INSIDE TRACK

| | |
|---|---|
| Who: | Anthony Chetti |
| What: | Elementary K–5 |
| Where: | San Diego, CA |
| Type of School: | Public (low socioeconomic status neighborhood; receives Title I funding and 98% of families qualify for free or reduced lunch) |

| | |
|---|---|
| How long: | 8 years |
| How much: | approximately $50,000 |
| Degree(s): | M.Ed. |
| School(s): | University of Florida (2000) |

### Insider Advice

Theory versus practicality. While attending an elementary education–teacher preparation program, at a college or university, a prospective teacher learns a great deal about how a good classroom is structured around individual student needs. These needs of the students are intended to drive the instruction that takes place in the classroom. Trying to implement this idea is not impossible, but is very challenging to do while also trying to adhere to state and/or district guidelines regarding curriculum, state standards and assessments. Children often suffer as the result of a mandated or so-called suggested pace of instruction. This pace of instruction is often hard to slow down. If a teacher does slow the pace and spends time reviewing concepts or reteaching, often these same students miss, or receive minimal exposure to, the total content, which they will then be tested on. These students too often are then bound to experience difficulty and failure. Not impossible to balance but very difficult, especially with decreased funding going to schools for the necessary supports and programs.

### What I Wish I Had Learned in School

How to implement behavior and classroom management techniques were not part of the curriculum, that I know of, at any college or university I have ever looked into. I suppose it is expected to be an innate part of the personality of those individuals who choose to teach in the classroom. However, I have seen many good teachers who received a degree and credential quit teaching due to their inability to manage groups of students. It is unfortunate that this was not addressed during their educational program, which should be designed to prepare them for teaching in the public school system.

### Greatest Joy

Seeing learning take place right before your eyes, because of your instruction.

### Biggest Drawback

All educators at all levels need to be respected and rewarded for their professionalism and efforts. Unfortunately, they continue to struggle to keep up with rising costs of living.

### Future Plans

To enter into administration, so that by sharing solid and proven instructional practices with other educators, more students can then be affected and receive a high quality public education.

# CHAPTER four

## GETTING CERTIFIED TO TEACH

**THE TEACHER** certification process is complex. This chapter guides you through the general requirements. It also includes state-by-state contact information for your department of education, so you can verify specific requirements.

Every profession has a way of guaranteeing that the people delivering a specialized service have the qualifications to perform that duty well. A license or certification provides that assurance—a means of quality control for professions like medicine, law, accounting, and education.

Because teachers mold the lives of children and have a tremendous impact on their students' future success in school and in life, ensuring that teachers are qualified is extremely important. Every state has a department of education that oversees the education and preparation of the teachers who work in that state. By providing this service, the state government assists local school districts in their search for qualified staff and sets minimum standards for all teachers across the state. The department also guarantees, to its constituents, that equally qualified teachers statewide provide education for the students from kindergarten through grade 12.

## THE TRADITIONAL ROUTE TO CERTIFICATION

Completing a teacher education program is only the first step in becoming a teacher. Then, you must fulfill all the requirements for the state in which you wish to teach, take the exam or exams required by the state, and officially apply for certification. Traditionally, to become a certified teacher, each person must complete the following steps. However, if you are a career changer or someone else who wants to find out about alternative routes to teacher certification, you may want to skip this section and go directly to the next section, "Alternative Routes to Certification."

### Step One: Obtain Your Degree

The first step in meeting the traditional certification requirements is to complete a program of study at an accredited college or university with an accredited department of education. To graduate, you will be required to complete a series of required courses, including practicums such as student teaching, and a series of elective courses that enrich your experience. If you pass these courses, then you can graduate and go on to take required tests and secure a teaching position. Regulations vary across the country, but all have the same purpose of guaranteeing uniformity of knowledge and preparation.

### Step Two: Meet Department of Education Requirements

Each state has its own department of education, which is responsible for verifying teachers' qualifications for certification. Each state requires that you complete a set of forms, pay application fees, and have background checks done. Listed below are some of the requirements you may have to meet when completing the application for certification.

## Citizenship
Many states require that applicants for certification be U.S. citizens, eligible for citizenship, or in the process of becoming a citizen. It is important for you to find this out before applying for a position. Of course, if you are a foreign exchange teacher (from a program abroad), this does not apply to you.

## No Criminal Record
Most states require fingerprinting, which is used to check for a criminal record. Some colleges and universities require this as part of their matriculation process. If you have had a problem that is believed to be in conflict with a teaching position, you will not be able to receive a teaching certificate. If you have had a problem, you should be honest about it. Have your college or university check this out for you—it is very possible that the situation can be straightened out before you apply for certification.

## Moral Character Reference
Some states require several letters of reference regarding your moral character. As a teacher, you will deal with children and young adults, so it is essential that you maintain high standards in your personal life. Your personal life history can have a lifelong impact on your professional goals.

## Recency Requirement
Some people do not begin to teach immediately after completing their teacher education program. If you were trained as a teacher but tried another career before going into the profession, you may have to provide evidence of taking courses within a specified period of time. This regulation also applies to teachers returning from a leave of absence or transferring to another state where they are requesting to be certified.

For more information on your state's certification requirements, look at The University of Kentucky's "Certification Requirements for 50 States" at http://www.uky.edu/Education/TEP/usacert.html. This project is a collection of the teacher certification requirements for all states, but keep in mind that states are continually revising their certification rules and requirements.

### Step Three: Written Tests

Many states require that you pass a competency test. Many states accept the Praxis series of exams, and some have their own tests, which are similar but may focus on specific needs of the state. Later in this chapter there is more information about the testing process and examples from the Praxis series.

### Step Four: Apply for Certification

Once you have met all the certification requirements for the state in which you want to teach, you can formally apply for certification. This normally means filling out an application and paying an application fee. In some states, the first certificate that is issued is provisional and you have to complete additional requirements before getting permanent certification.

## ALTERNATE ROUTES TO CERTIFICATION

In some cases, you don't actually have to be certified to be hired as a teacher. When the demand for teachers in a specific area is greater than the availability of licensed personnel, uncertified personnel can be hired through what is officially known as an *alternate route*; the state allows teachers to begin with minimum teaching requirements as long as they demonstrate competency in the subject area. Sometimes the teacher has to be in an approved education program (such as a master's program) or be under the mentorship of a master teacher. Requirements vary from state to state (and sometimes within a state) if there are extreme needs within a school system. Check with your state's department of education to see if they offer an alternative route to certification and to find out if you are eligible for one or more of their alternative programs.

In addition to alternative routes to teacher certification offered by specific states, you may be eligible for a national program.

## Teach for America

A national program recognized by most states, Teach for America is designed for college graduates who have not majored in education. It is a Peace Corps-like program that aims to eliminate educational inequity. The purpose of the two-year program is to attract bright scholars with varied interests into "hard-to-place" urban and rural school settings. Candidates are given a brief introduction to education methodology before beginning the service and are supported with professional development along the way. The hope for the program is ultimately to recruit and change the career paths of participants who would be headed into other fields. The program particularly aims to attract bilingual, science, and mathematics teachers. This program is a good way to get into the teaching field and can be a very rewarding—but trying—experience.

In 2009, applications surged 42%. With the economy and President Obama calling for community service, 35,000 college seniors applied for Teach For America. Competition is tough—less than 20% would be accepted.

## Troops to Teachers

A federally funded program, Troops to Teachers is designed to assist outgoing military personnel who want to work in the field of education. Within one year after being discharged from the service, an applicant may apply to become a teacher or a teacher's aide. Sometimes financial aid is available to defray the candidate's costs of education. The Troops to Teachers program also helps teachers find employment after completing the appropriate training.

## STATE LICENSING INFORMATION

Because the state—not federal—government regulates education, there are 50 versions of licensing requirements. You must find out what these requirements are for the state(s) in which you wish to teach so you can ensure that you are properly qualified. The directory of state departments of education at the end of this chapter provides contact information for all states.

## Categories of Licenses

The licensing systems of most states are divided into elementary, secondary specialty subjects, and K–12 specialty areas, including areas such as art, music, physical education, and sometimes special education. Often they are further divided into primary and middle school levels. In special education, some states have only one license for K–12, but others break special education down into specific disability categories.

## Dual Licenses

Each area of instruction requires a different course of study. To obtain dual licenses, you may have to take almost twice the number of courses, but it is usually worth the effort. Dual certification is a great benefit when you start to interview. A secondary teacher who is able to teach both social studies and English may be more desirable than one who can teach only one subject area. As enrollment increases, for example, class sections that do not require a full-time position may be added to a school schedule. A teacher with more than one specialty can sometimes fill two part-time positions.

At the elementary level, it is a bonus for a district to hire a teacher who has elementary certification and also is trained in reading and/or special education. In fact, any additional license often supports the first one. In addition, the person reviewing the hundreds of resumes submitted for consideration will look for something to differentiate candidates. Multiple certifications indicate that you can work with students who have disabilities (special education) or with students who are struggling to understand the required textbooks (reading specialist). In any case, it is something to consider when you are planning your course of study. Sometimes there is an overlap in requirements, and one teacher education course can count for two or three different certifications, which is a time and money saver for you as a student.

## The Final Phase—Obtaining a Full License

When you start teaching, you probably will not be fully licensed as a teacher. You will hold a nonrenewable, temporary, provisional, or limited certificate—the name and category depend on the state. The point is that some kind of initial license is granted to anyone who has a bachelor's degree and meets the other requirements discussed, but there are usually several more steps you must fulfill before you obtain a *full* (also known as a permanent or renewable) license. Most states require beginning teachers to demonstrate proficiency in the classroom over a period of three to five years. You must also demonstrate personal growth through the completion of additional courses; in fact, most states require you to complete a master's degree before you can be permanently certified. Some states even require that you continue to take continuing education courses to maintain your license. Each state has its own unique system for you to unravel.

## Reciprocity

Many states have reciprocal agreements for certification; that is, if you have attended school at an accredited college with an approved program in one state, you can probably use your transcripts to apply for a license in another state without taking all of the professional courses or the tests again. States with reciprocal agreements will accept your teaching credentials from another state and allow you to seek employment without additional schooling. However, sometimes a state will require one or more specialized courses or a qualifying exam before you can begin to teach. Others will allow you to begin to work but require you be enrolled in an appropriate course. Requirements vary, and it is up to you to find out exactly what you need to begin your first job.

## TEST TIME!

Each state has a unique list of requirements for certification. Several states have their own tests and others depend on the Educational Testing Service (ETS) and its Praxis Series of exams.

Some states require standardized exams that test your academic proficiency, such as the Praxis I: Academic Skills Assessment, which evaluates general knowledge in reading, writing, and mathematics. Similar state-specific tests are required in California and Texas. Instead of or in addition to these basic skills tests, many states test your professional knowledge using a test such as Praxis II: Subject Assessments, specific to your area of licensing. Some states also require Praxis III: Classroom Performance Assessments.

The Praxis Series was designed to develop a national minimum standard for all teachers who participate in this program. As with other tests designed by ETS, Praxis tests are carefully written to reflect the information they are seeking and normed across the country to provide a range of scores. State-specific tests are constructed with similar care. It is in your best interest to do as well as you can, because *interviewers will look at these scores*, and if they are forced to choose between equally dynamic candidates, the scale may tip toward the one with the better documented record of ability and information.

The information about the Praxis series that follows will be helpful to you not only if you have to take Praxis exams but also if you have to take a state-specific test, because there is some overlap among the tests.

## Praxis I: Academic Skills Assessment

The first test in the Praxis series measures basic reading, writing, and mathematics and can be taken in one of two formats. You can take the Computer-Based Test (CBT), administered by computer, whenever you can schedule an appointment. It is given throughout the year at many sites. You usually do not have to register in advance, and results are given immediately. The Pre-Professional Skills Test (PPST), the old-fashioned paper version, is given six times per year. Each subtest of the PPST is a one-hour multiple-choice test; however, the writing component also contains an essay, which you must complete in 30 minutes. The CBT also has these subtests, though the timing differs

The Praxis I often is given while you are in college. If you are beginning a second career, your college degree may replace this requirement for entrance into a graduate program.

## Reading

The first part of the Praxis I assessment measures your ability to read a passage and to demonstrate comprehension skills—identifying the main idea, finding specific information, and understanding the organization of the passage. It also measures your ability to analyze the passage, apply information, make inferences, and use words in context.

You are given a passage to read with specific questions to answer. The passages and questions vary in difficulty. For example, a nonfiction 100- or 200-word selection might be presented with many kinds of multiple-choice questions:

In this passage the author is primarily concerned with
  (A) explaining an event
  (B) making a comparison
  (C) listing facts
  (D) retelling a story
  (E) refuting an argument

Other multiple-choice questions include:

- Which of the following is an unstated assumption of the author?
- Which of the following statements bests expresses the author's main point of the passage?
- Which of the following best describes the organization of the passage?

As a teacher, you will be asking these kinds of questions of your students, and you must be well-versed in this area yourself!

## Writing

The second component of the Praxis I series is a writing test. It is divided into two parts: a multiple-choice segment and a writing sample. One kind of multiple-choice question is Error Recognition; you are asked to identify incorrect punctuation and word usage. You read a sentence or paragraph in which portions are underlined and lettered and then fill in the corresponding lettered space on the answer sheet to identify errors in grammatical relationships, mechanics, and idiom or word choice. You also may be asked to select a better way to state the given phrase or statement.

One such example follows:

The club member <u>agreed</u> that <u>each would contribute</u> ten days of volunteer work

                           A                        B

<u>annually</u> each <u>year at</u> the local hospital. <u>No error</u>.

   C           D                   E

There also is a series of multiple-choice questions called Sentence Correction, which require you to determine whether the underlined portion of the sentence or one of the other options is the best way to express the author's thought. Look at the following example:

Martin Luther King, Jr. <u>spoke out passionately</u> for the poor of all races.

    (A) spoke out passionately

    (B) spoke out passionate

    (C) did spoke out passionately

    (D) has spoke out passionately

    (E) had spoken out passionate

The second part of the Praxis I writing component is a writing sample. You must select one of two topics. The examiners are looking for your ability to "take a position on an issue" and support your point of view with solid reasoning and concrete examples. The writing component is scored holistically, from 1 to 6, where 1 is completely unacceptable and 6 is excellent. In our experience, a school district would have a hard time justifying the hiring of a teacher with a score lower than 4. You can do well on the test because you can plan ahead, write or think about the various topics, and then gather your supporting information or documentation.

One example of a question posed in this part of the test is, "Which of your possessions would be the most difficult for you to give up or lose? Discuss why." ETS offers free copies of *Tests at a Glance*, which gives examples of well and poorly written writing samples.

## Mathematics

The third component of the Praxis I series covers basic mathematical information that a student would learn by middle or junior high school. Many people forget some of these common equations (do you really remember how to multiply fractions or reduce to the lowest common denominator?). *You must prepare for this exam!* Concepts tested include place value, equivalent forms, sequence of operations, square roots, prime numbers, problem solving, algorithms, ratio, proportion, interpretation of data on charts and tables, measurement, geometry, systems, and logic.

Examples of mathematical questions posed include the following:

Some values of $x$ are less than 100. Which of the following is NOT consistent with the sentence above?

    (A) 5 is not a value of $x$

    (B) 95 is a value of $x$

    (C) Some values of $x$ are greater than 100

    (D) All values of $x$ are greater than 100

    (E) No numbers less than 100 are values of $x$

If $P \div 5 = Q$, then $P \div 10 =$

    (A) $10Q$

    (B) $2Q$

    (C) $Q \div 2$

    (D) $Q \div 10$

    (E) $Q \div 20$

## Praxis II: Subject Assessments

Completely separate from Praxis I, Praxis II is a series of tests (don't worry; you don't have to take them all) that measure content area knowledge. There are many variations of this test that match the many licenses available. If you want to become certified in only one area, you may have to take only one test; however, to become dually certified, you may have to take several.

One version of Praxis II is Principles of Learning, a case study approach that "measures a candidate's pedagogical knowledge" and is geared to grades K–6, 5–9, or 7–12. Many states ask for the Core Battery Tests, which can cover General Knowledge, Communication Skills, Professional Knowledge,

Multiple Assessments: Content Knowledge, or Multiple Assessments: Content Area. There are exams in the Praxis II series to certify every specialty you can think of—accounting, agriculture, early childhood education, health, every category of special education, English, reading, foreign language, music, mathematics, various levels of science instruction, and social studies. These tests often are required for certification in middle and high school curriculum areas.

Many of the Praxis II exams are constructed solely of more than 100 multiple-choice questions; the English Language, Literature, and Composition assessment, for example, has a content knowledge component with 150 multiple-choice questions and an essay component that requires several hours of writing. Each test is unique, and a state may require one, some, or none of these tests.

## How to Pass

You must invest time and effort into the process of test taking. Test taking is a skill, and the better prepared you are, the better your chances of doing well and passing. You also must study the content of the exam.

Use whatever materials you can find to help you study. Start with study guides, study tips, and free practice materials. Preview the types of questions you will be asked and the format of the assessments. You can usually obtain test prep material from your school of education or local libraries and bookstores.

### TEST TAKING TIPS

ETS offers some tips on how to pass its exams that will work equally well for *any exam* you have to take.

- Familiarize yourself with the test.
- Read the directions thoroughly and carefully.
- Try to understand the entire question before you respond.
- Pace yourself.
- Answer the easy questions first.
- Do not leave blank spaces; guess if you are not sure of an answer.
- Mark the answer sheet carefully.

- If it is a writing task, take notes and organize them before you begin the task.
- Review your responses for errors.

Remember that it is important to do well on standardized exams because they are part of the package that a prospective employer (a school district) will review when you apply for a job.

## Praxis III: Classroom Performance Assessments

The final test in the Praxis series, the Praxis III can be replaced by observations from your own administrator in many states. No matter how you would like to avoid this kind of evaluation, contracts are renewed, instructors are rehired, and teachers are granted tenure based on classroom observations. This test is used to assess various aspects of the new teacher's job performance.

## STATE DEPARTMENTS OF EDUCATION

The following pages contain a list of every state department of education, with their contact information. Requirements for most states are quite complex and change from time to time. Also, many states provide more than one route to meeting the requirements and will accept a teacher from out of state, particularly if that teacher has several years of full-time experience. You should be able to fine-tune the details needed for your license by contacting the department of education in your state for additional information.

### Alabama Teacher Education and Certification Office

http://www.alsde.edu
5201 Gordon Persons Building
P.O. Box 302101
Montgomery, AL 36130-2101
Phone: 334-242-9977

### Alaska Department of Education

http://www.eed.state.ak.us/TEACHERCERTIFICATION/

801 W. 10th Street, Suite 200

P.O. Box 110500

Juneau, AK 99811-0500

Phone: 907-465-2831

### Arizona Department of Education—Certification Unit

http://www.azed.gov/CERTIFICATION/

*Flagstaff Office*

2384 North Steves Boulevard, Box C

Flagstaff, Arizona 86004

Phone: 928-679-8117

*Phoenix Office*

P.O. Box 6490

Phoenix, AZ 85005-6490

602-542-4367

*Tucson Office*

400 W. Congress Street, #118

Tucson, AZ 85701

Phone: 520-628-6326

### Arkansas Department of Education

http://www.teacharkansas.org/

Office of Teacher Quality

501 Woodlane, Suite 220-C

Little Rock, AR 72201

Phone: 501-682-5535

### California Commission on Teacher Credentialing

//www.ctc.ca.gov/

P.O. Box 944270

1812 9th Street

Sacramento, CA 94244-2700

Phone: 1-888-921-2682

## Colorado Department of Education

http://www.cde.state.co.us/index_license.htm

201 E. Colfax Avenue

Denver, CO 80203

Phone: 303-866-6600

## Connecticut Department of Education

http://www.sde.ct.gov

165 Capital Avenue

Hartford, CT 06106-1630

Phone: 860-713-6543

## Delaware Department of Public Instruction

http://www.doe.k12.de.us/default.shtml

John G. Townsend Building

401 Federal Street

Dover, DE 19901

Phone: 302-739-4601

## District of Columbia

http://www.seo.dc.gov

Education Licensure Commission

441 4th Street, NW

Suite 350 North

Washington, DC 20001

Phone: 202-727-6436

## Florida Department of Education

http://www.fldoe.org/edcert/

Bureau of Teacher Certification

Turlington Building, Suite 1514

325 West Gaines Street

Tallahassee, FL 32399

Phone: 850-245-0505

### Georgia Professional Standards Commission

http://www.gapsc.com/

Two Peachtree Street, Suite 6000

Atlanta, GA 30303

Phone: 800-869-7775

### Hawaii Department of Education

http://doe.k12.hi.us/personnel/teachinginhawaii.htm

Teacher Recruitment Section

680 Iwilei Road, Suite 490

Honolulu HI 96817

Phone: 808-586-3420

### Idaho Department of Education

http://new.idahoeducationjobs.com/

650 W. State Street

P.O. Box 83720

Boise, ID 83720-0027

Phone: 208-332-6800

### Illinois Board of Education

http://www.isbe.state.il.us/certification/Default.htm

Division of Educator Certification

100 N. First Street

Springfield, IL 62777

Phone: 217-782-4321

### Indiana Department of Education

http://www.doe.in.gov/dps/welcome.html

Office of Licensing and Development

151 West Ohio Street

Indianapolis, IN 46204

Phone: 317-232-9010

## Iowa Department of Education

http://www.iowa.gov/boee/

Iowa Board of Educational Examiners

400 E. 14th Street

Des Moines, IA 50319-0146

Phone: 515-281-5294

## Kansas Department of Education

http://www.ksde.org

120 SE 10th Avenue

Topeka, KS 66612-1182

Phone: 785-296-3201

## Kentucky Department of Education

http://www.kyepsb.net/

Education Professional Standards Board

100 Airport Road, 3rd Floor

Frankfort, Kentucky 40601

Phone: 502-564-4606

## Louisiana Division of Teacher Certification and Preparation

http://www.doe.state.la.us/lde/tsac/home.html

Claiborne Building

1201 North 3rd Street

P. O. Box 94064

Baton Rouge , LA 70804-9064

Phone: 225-342-3490

## State of Maine Department of Education

http://www.maine.gov/education/cert/

Certification Office

23 State House Station

Augusta, ME 04333-0023

Phone: 207-624-6603

### Maryland State Department of Education

http://www.marylandpublicschools.org/msde/divisions/certification/certification_branch/

Certification Branch

200 W. Baltimore Street

Baltimore, MD 21201

Phone: 410-333-6442

### Massachusetts Department of Elementary and Secondary Education

http://www.doe.mass.edu/educators/e_license.html

75 Pleasant Street

Malden, MA 02148-4906

Phone: 800-439-2370

### Michigan Department of Education

http://www.michigan.gov/mde

608 W. Allegan Street

P.O. Box 30008

Lansing, MI 48909

Phone: 517-373-6791

### Minnesota Department of Education

http://cfl.state.mn.us/MDE/Teacher_Support/Educator_Licensing/index.html

Educator Licensing

1500 Hwy 36 West

Roseville, MN 55113

Phone: 651-582-8691

### Mississippi Department of Education

http://www.mde.k12.ms.us/ed_licensure/

Office of Educator Licensure

P.O. Box 771

Jackson, MS 39205-0771

Phone: 601-359-3513

Fax: 601-359-3033

## Missouri Department of Elementary and Secondary Education

http://dese.mo.gov/divteachqual/teachcert/

Teacher Quality and Urban Education

P.O. Box 480

Jefferson City, MO 65102-0480

Phone: 573-751-0051

## Montana Office of Public Instruction

http://www.opi.state.mt.us/

Educator Licensure

P.O. Box 202501

Helena MT 59620-2501

Phone: 406-444-3150

## Nebraska Department of Education

http://www.nde.state.ne.us/tcert/

301 Centennial Mall South

P.O. Box 94987

Lincoln, NE 68509-4987

Phone: 402-471-0739

## Nevada Department of Education

http://nvteachers.doe.nv.gov/

*Southern Nevada Office of Teacher Licensure*

9890 S. Maryland Parkway, Suite 231

Las Vegas, NV 89183

Phone: 702-486-6458

*Carson City Office of Teacher Licensure*

700 E. Fifth Street

Carson City, NV 89701

Phone: 775-687-9115

### New Hampshire Department of Education

http://www.ed.state.nh.us/education/beED.htm

Bureau of Credentialing

101 Pleasant Street

Concord, NH 03301-3860

Phone: 603-271-0052

### New Jersey Department of Education

http://www.nj.gov/education/educators/license/

Office of Licensing & Credentials

P.O. Box 500

Trenton, NJ 08625-0500

Phone: 609-292-2070

### New Mexico Department of Education

http://www.ped.state.nm.us/licensure/

Professional Licensure Bureau Education Building

300 Don Gaspar

Santa Fe, NM 87501-2786

Phone: 505-827-5821

### New York State Education Department

http://usny.nysed.gov/professionals/

Office of Teaching Initiatives

89 Washington Avenue

Albany, New York 12234

Phone: 518-474-3901

### North Carolina

http://www.dpi.state.nc.us/licensure/

State Department of Public Instruction

Licensure Section

6365 Mail Service Center

Raleigh NC 27699-6365

Phone: 1-800-577-7994

### North Dakota Education Standards and Practices Board

http://www.nd.gov/espb/

2718 Gateway Avenue, Suite 303

Bismarck, ND 58503-0585

Phone: 701-328-9641

### Ohio Department of Education

http://www.ode.state.oh.us/

Office of Educator Licensure

Ohio Departments Building

25 Front Street

Columbus, OH 43215-4183

Phone: 614-466-3593

### Oklahoma State Department of Education

http://sde.state.ok.us/

Hodge Education Building

2500 N. Lincoln Boulevard

Oklahoma City, OK 73105-4599

Phone: 405-521-3301

### Oregon Department of Education

http://www.tspc.state.or.us/

Teacher Standards and Practices Commission

465 Commercial Street NE

Salem, OR 97301

Phone: 503-378-3586

### Pennsylvania Department of Education

https://www.tcs.ed.state.pa.us/

Teacher Certification System

333 Market Street

Harrisburg, PA 17126-0333

Phone: 717-783-6788

### Rhode Island Department of Elementary and Secondary Education

http://www.ride.ri.gov/educatorquality/certification/

Office of Educator Quality and Certification

255 Westminster Street

Providence, RI 02903

Phone: 401-277-4600

### South Carolina Department of Education

http://www.scteachers.org/cert/index.cfm

Office of Educator Certification

3700 Forest Drive, Suite 500

Columbia, SC 29204

Phone: 803-734-8466

### South Dakota Department of Education

http://doe.sd.gov/teachers/

700 Governors Drive

Pierre, SD 57501-2291

Phone: 605-773-3134

### Tennessee State Department of Education

http://www.state.tn.us/education/lic/index.shtml

Office of Teacher Licensing

Tennessee Department of Education

4th Floor, Andrew Johnson Tower

710 James Robertson Parkway

Nashville, TN 37243

Phone: 615-532-4885

### Texas Education Agency

www.tea.state.tx.us

1701 N. Congress Avenue

Austin, TX 78701-1494

Phone: 512-463-9734

## Utah State Office of Education

http://www.schools.utah.gov/cert/

Educator Quality and Licensing

250 East 500 South

P.O. Box 144200

Salt Lake City, UT 84114-4200

Phone: 801-538-7510

## Vermont Department of Education

http://education.vermont.gov/

Educator Licensing

120 State Street

Montpelier, VT 05620-2501

Phone: 802-828-2445

## Virginia Department of Education

http://www.doe.virginia.gov/

Division of Teacher Education and Licensure

P.O. Box 2120

101 N. 14th Street

Richmond, VA 23218-2120

Phone: 804-292-3820

## Washington Office of Superintendent of Public Instruction

http://www.k12.wa.us/certification/

Professional Education and Certification Office

Old Capitol Building

P.O. Box 47200

600 Washington Street S.E.

Olympia, WA 98504-7200

Phone: 360-664-3631

**West Virginia Department of Education**

http://wvde.state.wv.us/index.html

Office of Professional Preparation

Building 6, Room 252

1900 Kanawha Boulevard, East

Charleston, West Virginia 25305-0330

Phone: 304-558-7010

**Wisconsin Department of Public Instruction**

http://dpi.wi.gov/tepdl/tm-license.html

125 S. Webster Street

P.O. Box 7841

Madison, WI 53707-7841

Phone: 800-441-4563

**Wyoming Department of Education**

http://ptsb.state.wy.us/

Professional Teaching Standards Board

1920 Thomes Avenue, Suite 400

Cheyenne, WY 82002

Phone: 307-777-6261

## THE INSIDE TRACK

| | |
|---|---|
| Who: | Caitlin Cassidy |
| What: | English Teacher, Theatre Director |
| Where: | Valley Stream North High School/Long Island, NY |
| Type of School: | Grades 7–12 |

| | |
|---|---|
| How long: | One year |
| How much: | $53,000 |
| Degree(s): | BA Theatre, BS Secondary Education for English/Communications |
| School(s): | Penn State University |

### Insider Advice

Let people help you! If experienced teachers offer assistance, take them up on the offer. Even if you don't really like them or their teaching style, you are going to gain something by listening to them, not to mention that they will probably let you borrow materials they have to help create lessons and give you ideas for units.

### What I Wish I Had Learned in School

Be prepared for the worst-case scenario. Sure, you may end up working at a school with a ridiculous amount of technology, but chances are the technology will have bad days, just like you will. Flexibility will keep you from becoming suicidal when the copier is broken (this happens more than I care to admit) or the SMART Board goes AWOL.

### Greatest Joy

That "aha!" moment when students finally understand something or think critically. Seeing the lightbulb go on above a student's head is priceless.

Another joy I have is when I am able to offer a fabulous retort to a student who is trying to ruffle my feathers. Yes, the student is young and should be expected to test her boundaries, but it still feels good to have a witty comeback. Plus, it usually means that she won't try to do it again, at least for another day or so.

### Biggest Drawback

Politics, both governmental and personal. Don't let yourself get bogged down with the issues people have with each other; just smile and nod, and let yourself decide.

### Future Plans

To find a school I love where I can help students discover themselves, become a fabulous teacher, and build a strong theatre program that makes kids want to come to school. I would also like to get my EdD at a prestigious university.

# CHAPTER five

## LET THE JOB SEARCH BEGIN

**JUST THE** idea of job hunting makes most people anxious. The options are overwhelming, and interviews with strangers can be intimidating. This chapter prepares you to approach this experience with confidence and professionalism, find the right job for you, and get hired! By the time you actually start to pound the pavement looking for your first teaching job, you have already made many decisions that make the process easier. You know that you want a teaching position. You know which certification(s) you hold and the qualifications needed to teach. Although you have not officially held a teaching position, you have been exposed to life in a classroom through internships and student teaching experiences and are well prepared for the job. Interviewers remember their own first interviews—an experience few people forget—and they understand your situation. As a beginning teacher, your experiences are justifiably limited, so you needn't be too intimidated. But how do you find the people who want to interview you?

Finding *the right job* requires intensive effort. Many positions may be available in your area of certification, so during the job search, application, and interview process, you must provide the proper information about yourself to ensure that the school district assigns a job that is a good match for you. In addition, you must find out about the school district to determine whether you are a good match for the job.

## FACTORS TO CONSIDER

Similar to the career and education choices you have made up to now, some of the decisions you make about your job will be according to your personal preferences; however, to be successful in the job search, you'll have to investigate some other choices. In Chapter One, we mentioned several factors that will affect your decision to apply for a job: kinds of school districts (rural, suburban, or urban; public or private settings) and issues such as salaries and benefits. Two more key factors that influence where you teach are geography, or location, and the availability of jobs in that area.

### Geography

Most people prefer to live and work in a particular location. It might as specific as a city, town, or school district or as vague as a region. Many teachers we know stay close to home or close to the college or university from which they graduated.

Look at maps and draw circles around areas you are willing to commute to and from. This will most likely be based on drive time, because quality of life is heavily affected by fighting traffic or spending too many hours on rural back roads. Next, drive around the areas of most interest to you to learn a lot about the community and school. Pay attention to your first reaction to the environment.

## Availability of Positions

One major factor that may affect your decision about where you want to teach is the availability of positions for your certification in a particular area. If you are certified to teach social studies but the demand for social studies teachers in your ideal area is low, you may have to consider moving to where the jobs are. Amy Gibbons, a certified elementary school teacher, moved from to New Jersey to Arizona to secure a job. The communities in Arizona were expanding, whereas the available elementary positions in New Jersey were decreasing.

## THE JOB MARKET TODAY

The education job market, like any job market, is a complicated and fluid environment driven by many factors. You have to keep the future in mind as you make decisions regarding employment. For example, if you are a beginning college student and want to be a teacher in a particular area, you must project four years into the future. If there is a shortage of secondary math teachers today, will it still be the case four years from now, when you are ready to enter the job market? Will the number of secondary math teachers who will graduate over the next three years meet or exceed demand?

The education job market is complex and driven by many internal and external forces. For example, a school district might increase the high school graduation requirements by adding one unit of credit in mathematics. This internal force will cause staffing needs to change, gradually but noticeably, in this school district because students will have to take more mathematics courses and fewer elective subjects. External forces also can affect staffing needs. A case in point is The Individuals with Disabilities Education Act (IDEA), and its predecessor, Public Law 94-142, which required school districts to offer special education students a free, appropriate education as governed by an Individual Education Plan (IEP). This legislation created many jobs for special education teachers and support services personnel.

## WHERE ARE THE TEACHING JOBS?

Because the market is continually changing, you need to take an active role in your job search. Sometimes, when a state or region's economy is in a slump, districts cut back on services that were not absolutely necessary. When this happens, districts often help already employed staff members become recertified so they can work in a specialty for which there is greater need. This results in fewer new jobs for new teachers.

To make yourself more marketable, write down the activities, classes, and electives that you've taught in the past. Or, make a separate list of activities, classes, and electives that you are interested in teaching. Create a master list you can pitch during an interview.

### Projected Trends

In its *Occupational Outlook Handbook*, the U.S. Bureau of Labor Statistics reports that growth is anticipated in the teaching field. The increase in the need for staff is projected from kindergarten through the secondary grades. Because some regions are instituting programs to improve early childhood education, such as offering full-day kindergarten and universal preschool, there will be many new jobs for preschool teachers; the expectation is that opportunities will be greater than the average for all occupations.

Student enrollment will drive the need for staff. Fast-growing states in the South and West—Nevada, Arizona, Texas, and Georgia—will experience the largest enrollment increases and have the most job opening for teachers. Enrollments in the Midwest are expected to hold relatively steady, while those in the Northeast are expected to decline.

The job market for teachers varies widely among states and school districts. Some urban cities and rural areas have difficulty attracting enough teachers, so job prospects should continue to be better in these areas than in suburban districts. Teachers in some subjects—mathematics, science and bilingual education, foreign language, for example—seem to be in short supply. Qualified vocational teachers also are currently in demand in a variety of fields at both the middle school and secondary school levels. Areas that seem to be experiencing an oversupply of teachers, on the other hand, include general elementary education, physical education, and social studies. Teachers who are geographically mobile and who obtain licensure in more than one subject should have a distinct advantage in finding a job.

## TEACHER SIGN-ON BONUSES

If your area of specialization is in math, science, foreign languages, or special education, you are at a distinct advantage because of the nationwide shortage of teachers in these areas. Your job search will be more about getting the best deal for you than about the best deal for the school. After you research some schools and find ones that you feel would be a good fit, you may want to investigate the perks they offer to lure new teachers into their schools. For example, some schools are handing out generous signing bonuses if you sign a contract to teach at their school, while others are offering gift certificates or other incentives to hire the teachers who are in demand.

## JOB SEARCH SQUARE ONE

Before you jump into your job search, get organized and be prepared. Being organized will make this research (or any research you do in your work or in life) so much easier!

Your first step in preparing your search is to get a calendar and devote it exclusively to your job search. It can be a regular paper calendar, or you can use your desktop scheduling software, such as Microsoft Outlook. Or maybe you have a Personal Digital Assistant (PDA), such as a BlackBerry. All of these are good choices, provided that you really commit yourself to using one of them and sticking with it.

If you use a paper calendar, get one that shows at least one week at a time. The calendar should be big enough for you to write clearly your job search schedule as well as any dates or events you need to keep track of during your search. If using an electronic calendar, make sure that you fill in necessary information and set reminders. You may even use the Task List function, which acts as an online to-do list.

Next, buy a box of manila folders from any stationery or office supply store. You can keep all relevant information for each job stored in its own folder.

Everything from job listings to notes to business cards can be kept on hand for easy access. Using folders is a sure way to keep yourself organized when busy.

Most teacher job postings will have the same type of information, so you may want to make an information sheet for each job listing where you can fill in the blanks for basic information. Here is a list of the information you should have available to you, at a glance, on one sheet:

- name of the school
- title of the position
- contact name
- job description
- skills needed
- educational requirements
- location
- salary
- benefits
- address, e-mail, or fax number where your resume should be sent
- date the job was posted
- date you (will) apply
- place where you found the job
- additional notes about the job

Keep in mind that finding a job *is* a type of job. As part of your preparation for your job search, you need to set a schedule. How much time? Be reasonable. You aren't going to be able to spend eight hours every day looking for a job, but you should aim for at least one to two hours every day. This isn't a requirement, but it is a good guideline to follow in order to maximize your chances for finding the right job. After all, new positions become available every day, so be consistent. Taking a few days off from the job search could cost you a position you really want. Also, find out if certain listings useful in your search are updated on a regular schedule. It won't help to look in your local paper on Friday if new classified listings are printed on Thursday.

## HOW TO FIND JOB OPENINGS

There are many ways to conduct a job search, but the most productive way is to combine the methods discussed in this section.

## College Placement Office and Education Department

The career placement office at your college or university is an excellent job-hunting resource. The placement office has brochures, books, and other data that can help direct your job search. In many placement offices, you can create a file containing your unofficial transcripts and letters of recommendation to send to prospective employers. Often, these services are also available to alumni, so if you've already graduated, consider calling the placement office to see if you can use their placement file service.

In addition, many teacher education departments receive job postings directly from school districts and provide a list of job openings at the local, regional, and state level to their students. Sometimes these listings will be posted on a bulletin board in plain view; in other schools you may need to ask the department secretary where to find them.

## Student Teaching or Substitute Experience

While you are student teaching or substitute teaching, be on the lookout for job vacancies that may open up in the school you are in. This is a great way to get hired full-time because the school administrators and other teachers can become familiar with your teaching skills and style. Try to develop good working relationships with everyone you meet during your student or substitute teaching experiences. You may be able to land a permanent position right at that very school, or another one in the district. You will have an advantage over your competition because you will already be familiar with the school's unique programs, needs, and culture. Even if a position doesn't open up while you are teaching there, if you keep in touch with a teacher or administrator at the school, you can find out when a position becomes available.

## Publications

Review job listings in publications from education organizations and other education-related publishers. *Education Week*, a weekly newspaper, has an extensive list of job openings in teaching and administration. Also check the local newspapers where you wish to teach; districts often list job openings in the local classified ads. Larger newspapers, such as the *New York Times*, publish a special section of education-related job openings (not part of the regular classified ads) every Sunday, in New York and nationwide. Become familiar with the format of the advertisements you read, so you can quickly find the information that is relevant to your own particular job search. While you can find teaching jobs advertised throughout the entire year, you will probably find that newspapers have the most teacher ads in them during the months of April through July.

## GIVE 'EM WHAT THEY WANT!

If you are answering an advertisement for a position, *follow all the directions* given in the ad. Include everything requested—copies of certification, self-addressed and stamped envelopes, letters of reference, and unofficial transcripts. Most applicants will be asked to complete applications right away, but if you don't submit everything as requested, your resume will end up in an "I'll get to it later pile" and will not be processed until someone gets around to calling you about the missing documentation.

## JOB FAIRS

Job fairs are becoming a popular way for public school districts to meet, and in some cases, hire on the spot, qualified teachers looking for work. In some cases, one school district will hold a job fair; in others, several school districts in one region will get together to sponsor a job fair. Each district sets up a booth where district representatives (human resources administrators, principals, and experienced teachers) provide employment applications and district information—such as salary schedules, class size, and projected vacancies—to prospective teachers. Job fair attendees can leave resumes and/or portfolios with the districts of their choice. Some districts conduct brief interviews during the job fair.

In addition to job fairs sponsored by school districts, many colleges and universities hold teacher placement days, usually in the spring of the year—these placement days are often called campus job fairs. As demand outstrips supply in certain areas of certification, some school districts are finding it necessary to travel to colleges in other states to recruit teachers. You may be able to meet with administrators or human resource directors from many different school districts at a campus job fair.

Both kinds of job fairs are an excellent source of information about available job openings in a particular area or region, and you can sometimes even get hired during a job fair. You can find out about job fairs from your college placement office, your college's education department, or your local newspaper.

To be successful on the job fair circuit, you should:

- Find the right job fair for you and your professional goals.
- Register in advance.
- Research the school districts that will have booths *before* you go.
- Write at least one fact about the school district that you found during your initial research that can be used to start the conversation.
- Create a time schedule, allowing yourself *at least* 10 to 15 minutes to spend at each booth.
- Dress professionally in clean, pressed, conservative clothing.
- Bring along your planner, writing materials, a folder, and some resumes. (You will be receiving lots of pamphlets and informational materials, as well *lots* of business cards, so keep everything together and organized.)
- Take notes about the people you meet, their names, their titles, or anything they tell you that stands out when you leave a booth.

After completing your entire agenda, leave some time to explore other opportunities.

Follow up by sending a letter to everyone you met whose address you obtained during the fair, restating your interest in the school and your qualifications for the position, as well as your interest in an on-site interview.

These job fairs are an excellent source of information about available openings in a particular area or region. First impressions *do* count, so you should look good and be professional. Our experience has shown that beginning teachers can make a positive and lasting impression on job fair recruiters. Because this meeting is very short, provide only the most critical information about yourself (name, certification, and job intent); do not review a portfolio of your undergraduate work—that will come later, in a formal interview. Leave a copy of your resume with the school official so an administrator in the school district can contact you later.

## Creating Your Own Network

Today's catchword is *networking*, which can be just as powerful and productive as more formal job searches. For a beginning teacher, though, the process is different than it will be after you have established a reputation in the profession. Your network includes:

- professional contacts made in the teacher education program
- friends and family, especially those who are in education-related jobs
- teachers and administrators who you met during your internship, student teaching, through tutoring, or through volunteering at schools
- friends and acquaintances from other settings such as religious, civic, and professional organizations and social clubs

It pays to get to know as many professionals in your field as possible. Work with them, and do your best to impress them. You might meet other teachers at workshops, conferences, and classes—make it a priority to get their contact information for the future. It also helps to get into a school district and accept whatever position is open at the time, even as a teacher's aide or as a substitute teacher. After you have made a good impression on other teachers and principals, you are in a good position to apply for a full-time position.

An elementary teacher adds, "I really think networking is the best way to find a job. People who know you and know your work can give you good and realistic advice on schools, and they can also speak on your behalf. I know that a lot of teaching jobs come about this way; in fact, I got my most recent job by networking. I spread the word to everyone I could think of that I was looking for a job, so as many people as possible knew about it."

How many times have you heard the statement, "It is not *what* you know, but *who* you know"? There is comfort and security in hiring someone you know or who is familiar to your colleague. The reality is that it can be advantageous to know *the right people*, or those who can help you get an interview for the position you want. Tell people that you are looking for a teaching job, ask them to pass your name along, or ask whether they know of any available teaching positions. Try connecting online with services like Facebook and LinkedIn. Ask these people for permission to use their names as references. Networking may help you get an interview and, ultimately, a job.

## Online Job Searches

One of the best resources for job hunters is the Internet. There's no one best website for looking for a job. A good hint is to find three or four sites that work best for you and check those regularly.

You may have heard of some of the most popular job searching websites, such as monster.com. These sites boast millions of visitors every year and list hundreds of thousands of job openings for all different types of careers. These mega sites offer education listings that can be searched by locality and other search criteria.

Other websites are specifically geared for teachers. Several examples of websites where you can post your resume and view job postings specifically geared for teachers and other education professionals are:

http://www.teachers-teachers.com. Teachers-Teachers.com offers a job placement service for teachers. You can register to use their resume builder to create an online version of your resume. Then, you can list your job specifications, indicating in which states, subjects, and type of school (public/private) you would like to teach. If there are job openings that match your specifications, you will receive an e-mail notification. If you find a job opening that appeals to you, you can log on to your personal home page on their site to more thoroughly view the open position. From there, you can click on a school's name to view their website. If you want to apply for a job, you can save your cover letter online and e-mail it with the click of a button. The site is affiliated with the American Association of Colleges for Teacher Education.
http://www.k12jobs.com. This site lists job postings at kindergarten, elementary, junior high, and high schools. Each job posting includes school name, location, application deadline, salary, contact information,

and the school's e-mail and website addresses. You can search by job title, category, school name, or state that the job opening is located in.

**http://www.cec.sped.org/cc/cc.htm.** CEC Career Connections is operated by The Council for Exceptional Children (CEC) and claims that it is the only job bank on the Internet devoted exclusively to special education professionals. This Internet Job Posting Service is an online bulletin board listing job vacancies. Employers post job vacancies on the Internet-based job bank that is accessible only through the CEC website. The Resume Referral Service is a database of resumes that employers can search to find appropriate applicants. Job seekers can gain access to the database and search it by geographical location, job title, or other key words. There is no fee for searching the database.

**http://www.hireed.net.** You can use HireEd.net to post your resume, search job openings online, and even set up a search agent so that HireEd.net will conduct automatic searches and notify you via e-mail about job postings that match your qualifications and interests. HireEd.net's Job Seeker services are free for all members of the Association for Supervision and Curriculum Development (ASCD). If you're not a member, you can still post your resume and search the job listings at no charge—but you will be charged a fee for setting up a search agent and having HireEd.net search for jobs for you. To get started, click on Job Seeker on the page's left-hand scroll bar, register, and begin your job search.

**www.teacherjobs.com.** This educational placement service places educators in public, private, and parochial schools on the elementary, secondary, and college levels throughout the nation. It claims to be "the largest teacher placement service in the United States." While there is no registration fee or cost to use this placement service, there is a fee if you land a job through a contact gained from their service. So, if you secure employment through information provided by their company, you will pay a fee (usually a percentage of your first year's salary.)

**http://www.edweek.org/jobs.cfm.** This site is the Marketplace section of *Education Week* on the Web. The marketplace consists of a wide range of administrative and teacher vacancies across the United States and abroad. You can browse through the ads by region or by job title. These listings are updated weekly and provide you with all the information you need to apply for a position. Many of the nation's top school districts, universities, and educational organizations advertise in the Marketplace. You can browse their listings for free.

**http://careers.education.wisc.edu/ProjectConnect/MainMenu.cfm.** To access teaching vacancies at *Project Connect: Connecting Schools and Teachers in the Information Age*, you need to get a username and password from the college or university where you received your teacher education degree. You can search the website address listed above to find state-by-state listings of educational institutions to see if your college is connected.

**http://www.education-world.com/jobs.** This education employment center offers free services for those seeking teaching jobs; you can browse job listings and other people's posted resumes as well as submit your own resume online.

**http://www.greatteacher.net.** Click on the link "Job Classifieds" to see a listing of available jobs. Positions are categorized by location (state, country, or region) and can be found in the category scroll-down box under "Select A Location." Each ad has a job description along with contact information. When you click the "contact" button, a response form appears which can be e-mailed directly to the employer by clicking "send."

**http://www.school-jobs.net.** This site offers a bulletin board where job seekers and schools can find each other. You can search job openings nationwide by salary, location, or area of expertise. When you find a position that interests you, you can contact the school directly to apply. In addition, you can post your resume at no charge on this site. If a school is interested in your resume, they will contact you directly.

**http://www.ihiresecondaryteachers.com.** This job posting site is free to prospective teachers. You must register as a new candidate and complete the profile information in order to view the job ads. You apply for a job based on the information supplied in the ad. The employer may then respond if interested. After you have registered, completed the profile, and submitted your resume, iHire will send you an e-mail when you have been matched to a position. You can then return to the website and log in. When you arrive at the candidate menu page, select "view potential job matches" to see the list of matched jobs. Click on the job ID#

and the job information will appear. If you would like to apply for a position, answer the requirement section and hit the "submit" button. This will allow the employer to view your application and resume. Job ads are posted for 60 days only. The employer has three options when reviewing your resume—keep it under review, disapprove it, or send you an e-mail notification to contact them for an interview. The status will be listed next to the job ID# on your list of jobs responded to.

## PREPARING YOUR RESUME

Once you determine where the jobs are, contact the district(s) in which you would like to teach. The usual way to make this contact is to send a cover letter and a resume, which is a written summary about your experience and academic preparation. As in face-to-face meetings, *first impressions count*, and a resume must make a good impression on the reader immediately. One principal in a small midwestern high school initially sorted resumes into two piles to determine which ones to review more closely. Any resume that contained the slightest mistake in spelling or grammar, had typographical errors, or was excessively long was considered unacceptable. Knowing the appropriate format and critical information to include on a resume will not guarantee that you get an interview; however, not presenting yourself professionally in writing generally means disaster. A teacher is a professional, and your resume should reflect professionalism.

No matter what type of resume you're creating, here are some useful tips and strategies that will help ensure that your finished document has the most impact possible when a potential employer reads it.

- Always use standard letter-size ivory, cream, or neutral-color paper. Brightly colored papers do not copy well and look unprofessional.
- Include your name, address, and phone number on every page if you use more than one page.
- Make sure your name is larger than anything else on the page (example: your name in 14-point font, the rest in 12 point).
- Use a font that is easy to read, such as 12-point Times New Roman, Century Schoolbook, or Ariel.

- Do not use more than one font in your resume. You want it to look like a resume, not a ransom note.
- Be consistent when using bold, capitalization, underlining, and italics. If one company name is underlined, make sure all are underlined. Check titles, dates, and so on.
- Edit, edit, edit. Read it forward and backward. Have friends with good proofreading skills read it. Even if you have a grammar and spellchecker on your computer, you still need to review it. For instance, a spellchecker would not catch any of the errors in the following sentence: *Their are two many weighs too make errors that a computer does nut recognize.*
- Use bullet points for items in a list. If someone is glancing at your resume, it helps highlight the main points.
- Use keywords in your industry.
- Avoid using excessive graphics such as boxes, distracting lines, and complex designs.
- Don't list your nationality, race, religion, birth date, marital status, or gender. Keep your resume as neutral as possible. Your resume is a summary of your skills and abilities.
- One page is best, but do not crowd your resume. Shorten the margins if you need more space; if it's necessary to create a two-page resume, make sure you balance the information on each page. Don't put just one section on the second page. Be careful about where the page break occurs.
- Keep your resume updated. Don't write "12/08 to present" if you ended your job two months ago. Do not cross out or handwrite changes on your resume.
- Understand and remember everything written on your resume. Be able to back up all statements with specific examples.

To ensure that your resume will be serious considered by a potential employer, avoid making these common errors:

- Stretching the truth. A growing number of employers are verifying all resume information. If you're caught lying, you won't be offered a job, or you could be fired later if it's discovered that you weren't truthful.

- Including any references to money unless specifically instructed to. This includes past salary or how much you're looking to earn.
- Including on your resume the reasons why you stopped working for an employer, switched jobs, or are currently looking for a new job. Also, do not include a line in your resume saying, "unemployed" or "out of work" along with the corresponding dates in order to fill a time gap.
- Having a typographical or grammatical error in a resume. If you refuse to take the time necessary to proofread your resume, why should an employer assume you'd take the time needed to do your job properly if you're hired?
- Using long paragraphs to describe past work experience. Consider using short sentences, phrases, or a bulleted list instead. Most employers will spend less then one minute initially reading a resume.

## WHAT YOUR RESUME SAYS ABOUT YOU

Most potential employers want to know the same basic things about you: your name, address, education, certification, and work experience. You might also include your specific job objective, the professional organizations you belong to, and your professional references.

Even if you choose to hire a professional resume writer or resume preparation service to create your resume, he or she will require the majority of this information in order to do a good job creating a resume on your behalf. The same holds true if you purchase off-the-shelf resume creation software for your computer. Keep in mind, the majority of these resume writing tips and strategies apply to traditional printed resumes as well as to electronic resumes that you submit online.

The first section of any resume includes information about how a potential employer can contact you. The details you will want to provide include contact information, job objective(s), work/employment history, and references.

### Contact Information

- full name _____
- permanent street address _____

- city, state, zip _____
- daytime telephone number_____
- evening telephone number_____
- pager/cell phone number (optional) _____
- fax number (optional) _____
- e-mail address _____
- school address (if applicable) _____
- your phone number at school (if applicable) _____

If you live at school or if you are thinking of moving soon, include a permanent address as well as your current information.

Do not include personal information in the resume. You could endanger your chances of getting hired if you include information about your religion, marital status, race, or other personal details.

The following questions will help you pinpoint the specific types of information that needs to go into the various sections of your resume and/or cover letter. By answering these questions, you will also get to know yourself better, so you can find the job opportunities you will prosper in and that you will enjoy.

## Job Objective(s)

Many resumes begin with a career goal or objective. It doesn't have to be profound or philosophical; just list the job you want to obtain. The purpose of the objective is to assure potential employers that they are about to read a relevant resume.

In the space that follows, write a short description of the job you're seeking. Be sure to include as much information as possible about how you can use your skills to the employer's benefit. Later, you will condense this answer into one short sentence.

What is the job title you're looking to fill (e.g., elementary teacher)?

### NOW STARRING . . .

Your degree(s) and certification(s) are the stars of your resume. Make sure they are easy to find (that is, located near the beginning of the resume) and clearly written.

The first things that a personnel director, supervisor, or principal hiring a new employee looks for on a resume are the degree(s) and certification(s) of the applicant. How the applicant's information matches the hiring needs determines whether the remaining information on the resume will be read.

## Educational Background and Certification

List the specific type(s) of certification you have and the state(s) in which that certification was granted:_____

_____

When listing your educational background, start with your most recent school and work backward. List your degree or certificate, the name and location of the school, and the date you graduated. Also include special programs or teacher-related continuing education courses you have completed.

List the most recent college or university you've attended:_____

_____

City/State: _____

What year did you start?_____

Graduation month/year: _____

Degree(s) and/or award(s) earned: _____

Your major(s):_____

Your minor(s):_____

List some of your most impressive accomplishments, extracurricular activities, club affiliations, and so on:_____

_____

_____

_____

List specialized education courses you've taken that help qualify you for the job you're seeking: _____

_____

Grade point average (GPA): _____

Other college/university you've attended:_____

City/State:_____

What year did you start? _____

Graduation month/year: _____

Degree(s) and/or award(s) earned: _____

Your major(s):_____

Your minor(s): _____

List some of your most impressive accomplishments, extracurricular activities, club affiliations, and so on:_____

_____

List specialized education courses you've taken that help qualify you for the job you're seeking: _____

_____

Grade point average (GPA): _____

High school attended: _____

City/State: _____

Graduation date: _____

Grade point average (GPA): _____

List the names and phone numbers of two or three current or past professors, teachers, or guidance counselors you can contact about obtaining a letter of recommendation or list as references: _____

_____

## Work/Employment History

List all your experience working with children, even if it isn't specifically as a teacher, such as summers spent as a mother's helper. For career changers, also list all managerial experience you have; every job requires skills interacting with people. Summer employment or part-time work should be labeled as such, and you will need to specify the months in the dates of employment for positions you held for less than a year.

If you just finished your teacher education program, you might feel like you don't have much experience to list in a resume. This is not true! Think back to those grueling college projects. Getting a grade on a project was only half the project's value. You can use it now in place of experience you have not yet gained in the workplace. List special projects with their title, a description, and lessons learned.

Most recent employer: _____

City, State: _____

Year you began work: _____

Year you stopped working (write "Present" if still employed): _____

Job title: _____

Job description: _____

_____

Reason for leaving: _____

_____

_____

What were your three proudest accomplishments while holding this job?

1. _____

2. _____

3. _____

Contact person at the company who can provide a reference: _____

_____

Contact person's phone number: _____

Annual salary earned:_____

For special school projects, list the title of the project:_____

Description of special project:_____

_____

Lessons learned from project:_____

_____

_____

Employer:_____

City, State:_____

Year you began work:_____

Year you stopped working: _____

Job title: _____

Job description: _____

_____

Reason for leaving: _____

_____

_____

What were your three proudest accomplishments while holding this job?

1. _____

2. _____

3. _____

Contact person at the company who can provide a reference:_____

_____

Contact person's phone number: _____

Annual salary earned:_____

For special school projects, list the title of the project: _____

_____

Description of special project: _____

_____

Lessons learned from project: _____

_____

_____

## Military Service (if applicable)

Branch of service you served in: _____

Years served: _____

Highest rank achieved: _____

Decorations or awards earned: _____

Special skills or training you obtained:_____

## Professional Organizations

List any professional organizations that you are a member of:_____

_____

_____

_____

## Hobbies and Special Interests

List any hobbies or special interests you have that are not necessarily work-related, but that potentially could separate you from the competition. Can any of the skills utilized in your hobbies be used for coaching or leading any extracurricular activities at a school?

_____

_____

What non-professional clubs or organizations do you belong to or actively participate in? _____

_____

_____

## References

References are an increasingly important part of a resume. Individuals who are responsible for and directly in contact with students must be carefully screened, so your _references will be contacted_. Give some thought to the three to five individuals who you list as references. These individuals must be able to attest to your character and to your ability to teach, so select them with care. In some cases, school districts do not expect references to be listed on the resume; at the end of your resume, add "References are available upon request."

Because of the risk of possible repercussions, already employed applicants might not want their current employer contacted until the school district expresses interest in offering employment. If the district requires you to list references and you do not want them contacted early in the interview process, note that fact on the resume or in the cover letter. If there is no reason why your references cannot be contacted at any time, then including them with your resume may expedite your consideration as a prospective applicant. Some personnel directors or administrators may want to call your references before the interview, whereas others may wait until after they have met you.

## PERSONAL/PROFESSIONAL AMBITIONS

Take some time to reflect on the questions in this section; your answers to many of these questions can help you not only in the preparation of your resume but also in your broader career planning activities.

What are your long-term goals?_____

Personal: _____

_____

Professional: _____

_____

For your personal and professional goals, what are five smaller, short-term goals you can begin working toward achieving right now that will help you ultimately achieve each of your long-term goals?

Short-Term Personal Goals

    1. _____

    2. _____

    3. _____

    4. _____

    5. _____

Short-Term Professional Goals

    1. _____

    2. _____

    3. _____

    4. _____

    5. _____

Will the job(s) you will be applying for help you achieve your long-term goals and objectives? If yes, how? If no, why not?

_____

_____

Describe your personal and professional situation right now: _____

_____

_____

_____

What would you most like to improve about your life overall? _____

_____

_____

What are a few things you can do, starting immediately, to bring about positive changes in your personal or professional life? _____

_____

_____

Where would you like to be personally and professionally five and ten years down the road? _____

_____

_____

What needs to be done to achieve these long-term goals or objectives? ___

_____

_____

_____

What are some of the qualities about yourself, your appearance, and your personality that you're most proud of? _____

_____

_____

What are some of the qualities about yourself, your appearance, and your personality that you believe need improvement? _____

_____

_____

What do others most like about you? _____

_____

_____

What do you think others least like about you? _____

_____

_____

If you decided to pursue additional education, what would you study and why? How would this help you professionally? _____

_____

_____

_____

If you had more free time, what would you spend it doing? _____

_____

_____

_____

List several accomplishments in your personal and professional life that you're most proud of. Why did you choose these things?

_____

_____

_____

_____

_____

What do you believe is your biggest weakness? Why wouldn't an employer hire you?

_____

_____

_____

What would be the ideal atmosphere for you to work in? Do you prefer a large public school atmosphere, or a small private school campus? _____

_____

_____

_____

List five qualities about a new job that would make it the ideal teaching assignment for you:

1. _____

2. _____

3. _____

4. _____

5. _____

What did you like most about the last place you worked? _____

_____

What did you like least about the last place you worked?_____

_____

What work-related tasks are you particularly good at?_____

_____

_____

What type of students would you prefer to have? _____

_____

_____

When it comes to work-related benefits and perks, what's most important
to you? _____

_____

_____

When you're recognized for doing a good job, how do you like to be rewarded?_____

_____

_____

If you were to write a help wanted ad describing your ideal teaching job,
what would the ad say? _____

_____

_____

Using the information in the previous questionnaire, you should be able to begin piecing together content for your resume. Whatever you do, however, never simply copy your resume right out of a book. Use the sample resumes provided in this book and in other resume books as a guide, but be sure the content is 100% accurate and customized to you.

## POWER WORDS

The following short list contains examples of skill-related words and phrases you could incorporate into your resume (assuming they are skills you actually have):

| | | |
|---|---|---|
| analyzing | designing | record keeping |
| coaching | innovating | researching |
| communicating | motivating | scheduling |
| consulting | negotiating | supervising |
| coordinating | organizing | teaching |
| counseling | performing | training |
| creating | planning | writing |
| data entry | public speaking | |

## THE ELECTRONIC RESUME

If you plan to use the Internet to apply for teaching jobs, your resume will require special formatting so it can be read electronically.

An electronic resume can be created and distributed in a variety of ways. Remember that, there are no standard guidelines to follow when creating an electronic resume, since employers use different computer systems and software. Thus, it's important that you adhere to the individual requirements of each online job site you visit—use their specific formatting, saving, and sending formats when at their site. The majority of employers who work with online job services prefer to receive resumes in PDF format, however, some may accept .doc files (documents saved in Word format), for example.

In order to keep incoming resumes consistent in terms of formatting, many websites designed for recruiting insist that all electronic resumes be created using a predefined template. While online, you can complete a detailed form that requests all pertinent resume information. You will be prompted for each piece of information separately in predefined fields. The website then formats the information automatically to meet the employer's requirements.

When completing an online-based resume form, be sure you fill in all fields with the appropriate information only. Be mindful of limitations for each field. For example, a field that allows for a job description to be entered may have space for a maximum of only 50 words, so the description you enter needs to provide all of the relevant information (using keywords), but also be written concisely. Since an electronic resume is as important as a traditional one, consider printing out the online form first and then spend time thinking about how you will fill in each field (or answer each question).

Don't attempt to be clever and try adding information that wasn't requested in a specific field in order to provide more information about yourself. For example, if you're only given space to enter one phone number, but you want to provide a home and cell phone number, don't use the fields for your address to enter the second phone number.

Be sure to proofread your electronic resume carefully before hitting the send button. Just as with a traditional resume, spelling mistakes, grammatical errors, or providing false information won't be tolerated by employers. When creating an electronic resume to be saved and submitted, follow these general formatting guidelines:

- Set the document's left and right margins to display 6.5-inches of text per line. This will ensure that the text won't automatically wrap to the next line (unless you want it to).
- Use a basic, 12-point text font, such as Courier or Times Roman.
- Avoid using bullets or other symbols. Instead of a bullet, use an asterisk or a dash. Instead of using the percent sign for example, spell out the word percent. (In your resume, write 15 percent, not 15%).
- If one is available, use a spellchecker to help you proofread your electronic resume and then proofread the document carefully yourself.
- Avoid using multiple columns, tables, or charts within your document.
- Within the text, avoid abbreviations—spell everything out. For example, use the word *Director*, not *Dir.*, or *Vice President* as opposed to *VP*. In terms of degrees, however, it's acceptable to use terms like MBA, BA, and PhD.

Properly formatting your electronic resume is important; however, what you say within your resume is what could ultimately get you hired. Keywords are the basis of the electronic search and retrieval process. Keywords are nouns and phrases that highlight your professional areas of expertise; they include industry-related jargon, projects, achievements, special task forces, and other distinctive features about your work history.

Select and organize your resume's content in order to highlight those keywords. The idea is to identify all possible keywords that are appropriate to your skills and accomplishments that support the kind of job you are looking for. But to do that, you must apply traditional resume writing principles to the concept of extracting those keywords from your resume. Once you have written your resume, then you can identify your strategic keywords based on how you imagine people will search for your resume.

The keywords you incorporate into your resume should support or be relevant to your job objective. Some of the best places within your resume to incorporate keywords is when listing:

- job titles
- responsibilities
- accomplishments
- skills

Industry-related buzzwords, job-related technical jargon, licenses, and degrees are among the other opportunities you will have to come up with keywords to add to your electronic resume.

Keywords are the backbone of any good electronic resume. If you don't incorporate them, your resume won't be properly processed by the employer's computer system. Choosing the right keywords to incorporate into your resume is a skill that takes some creativity and plenty of thought. Instead of using action verbs, use nouns or adjectives to describe your skills, job responsibilities, and qualifications. For example, instead of using the action word *managed*, use *manager* or *management*. Also, be sure to include the keywords listed by the employer within the job description or help wanted ad you're responding to.

## SAMPLE RESUMES

Two examples of teacher resumes follow for your reference. Look carefully at the first one. This resume does not adequately communicate the candidate's ability to be a teacher. Shonda's objective is nebulous, her teaching experience and activities reveal very little about her knowledge and skills, and her format (including type and organization) does not enhance her image as a professional. Perhaps most importantly, Shonda has buried her certifications in the middle of her resume where they are hard to find.

Although the second resume is not perfect, it more accurately portrays the abilities of the candidate. A personnel director scanning Jose's resume knows exactly which position he is applying for and what his qualifications are. More important, Jose has described his experience to demonstrate that he can work with a variety of constituents in a school setting. He also is creative and can bring his ideas to reality. Jose's resume will definitely make a more favorable impression than Shonda's will.

### A Less-Than-Convincing Sample Resume

Shonda Smith
15 Allemeda Blvd.
Anywhere, Pennsylvania 54321

*OBJECTIVE:* To become a leader for today and tomorrow
*TEACHING EXPERIENCE:*
    Student Teaching, Anywhere, PA, Schools, 2006
    Summer School Volunteer Teacher, Anywhere, PA, Schools, 2005
*EDUCATION:*
    *University of Pennsylvania, B.S. in Education, 2007*
*ACTIVITIES:*
    *Member—Student National Education Association*
    Member—Delta Delta Delta
*HONORS:*
Collegiate Academic All-American, Who's Who in American Education, Future Leaders in Education Meeting Invitee and Dean's List—USC.
*AREAS OF CERTIFICATION:*
    English (K–6), Special Reading (K–12), and BD (K–8)

*PROFESSIONAL WRITINGS:*
   *Understanding the BD student in the Regular Classroom* (published).
*REFERENCES:*
   Available upon request

### A High-Quality Sample Resume
### Jose Rivera
5555 S. Hope Street
Anywhere, Nebraska 12345
(555) 555-5555

## CAREER OBJECTIVE
Secondary English Teacher

## CERTIFICATION
English, 7–12
Reading, K–12

## EDUCATION
| | |
|---|---|
| B.S. in Education | University of Nebraska–Lincoln, 2008 |
| Blaine High School | Anywhere, Nebraska, 2004 |

## EXPERIENCE
**Student Teacher**, Glendale High School, September 2007–January 2008
Worked with courses in grades 9, 11, and 12.
Planned and implemented units on English literature and writing.
**University of Nebraska–Lincoln**, Student Teacher Advisory Committee
Created orientation and debriefing sessions for students beginning and completing their student teaching assignments.
**Blaine High School**, Student Assistance Team Counselor
Planned and directed weekly meetings with administrators, teachers, and students promoting a drug-free school.
Revised the high school's drug-free student's manifesto.
**Blaine High School**, Site Council
Chaired a subcommittee for improving the learning environment that implemented ideas to lessen class disruptions and increase time on task.

## REFERENCES
Available upon request

## THE COVER LETTER

In a nutshell, a cover letter is your initial introduction to a potential employer. It should get the recipient interested—and even excited—to read your resume.

As a general rule, never submit your resume to a potential employer unless it is accompanied by a personalized cover letter. Think of the cover letter as a companion document to your resume. This specialized form of the basic business letter is designed to:

- introduce you to a potential employer
- state what job you are applying for
- explain some of the reasons why your resume is worth looking at
- request some sort of action to be taken by the reader, such as inviting you for an interview

Here are some points to remember as you write your cover letter:

- Use a professional business letter format.
- Quickly introduce yourself and explain your reason for writing.
- State how you found out about the position.
- Be brief, but show that you know something about the position; express interest in the position and describe how your abilities match the qualifications for the position.
- Demonstrate that you know something about the school district.
- Indicate that you would like to come in for a formal interview.
- Proofread the letter for spelling, grammar, and typing errors.

Always keep the purpose of your writing in mind; it will direct your thoughts and keep you on task. Write concisely, clearly, and directly, and do not overuse the passive tense. Follow the old rule of speaking, and adapt it to your writing: Tell them why you are writing, write about it, and then summarize it.

Whether you are creating a cover letter that will be printed out, then hand-delivered, mailed, or faxed (as opposed to e-mailed along with an electronic resume), the content and format of the cover letter is the same. The only difference between the two is that an electronic cover letter will be placed in the main body of an e-mail message, typically with your resume as an attached file.

The cover letter will have the following distinct parts:

- your contact information
- their contact information
- date
- salutation
- opening paragraph
- primary message paragraph(s)
- supporting paragraph
- specific request for action
- closing
- enclosure

Before you actually sit down to write a cover letter, make sure you know:

- recipient's full name
- recipient's job title
- company name
- company mailing address
- the exact position you are applying for

An example of a good cover letter follows.

## SAMPLE COVER LETTER

Your name
5555 S. Hope Street
Anywhere, Nebraska 12345

April 13, 2008

Dr. John Dunn
555 South Benton
Klamath Falls, Oregon 56789

re: English teacher position

Dear Dr. Dunn:

I am applying for the position of secondary English teacher at Rodeo High School. I learned about this position at the University of Oregon Career Placement Day, held in early April. I believe my education, experiences, and interests meet the expectations for this position.

This position requires someone with not only excellent credentials to teach English but also excellent writing skills. My resume shows that I have been published in a variety of journals and that I have conducted many workshops for other college students on ways to improve their writing skills. I also served as a volunteer student tutor in a learning center for at-risk students at a local high school. Documentation of these students' work indicates substantial improvement in their grades when they returned to traditional English courses.

While in high school and college, I was very active in a variety of organizations and activities. These experiences complement my academic preparation. I would be very interested in sponsoring student activities in your school.

I believe my academic preparation, school-related activities, and career goals match the requirements for this position. I am confident that I will be an asset to your school and that this position can fulfill my professional and personal needs as well. I am hoping to hear from you soon to schedule an appointment for an interview. Please call me at (555) 555-5555.

Thank you for considering my qualifications.

Sincerely,
Jose Rivera
enclosure: resume

## FILLING OUT AN APPLICATION

If you are asked to complete an application, follow the rules for writing a resume. Here are some additional pointers:

- If you hand write your application, *do it neatly!*
- If you are a good typist, type the application, so it will be easier to read.
- Answer every relevant question.
- List as many references as are requested.
- List hobbies, if asked. They may correspond to extracurricular activities in the school.
- Answer questions in complete sentences.
- If you are given a page to write your philosophy of education, use the entire page. Explain why you responded the way you did. Support your answer with experiences and facts.

Your writing is a mirror of who you are, so be careful and thoughtful in your response!

## THE INTERVIEW: HIGH ANXIETY

There is so much at stake professionally and financially in your first interview that you probably will be very nervous. In fact, few other experiences produce such high levels of anxiety. To complicate the situation, many people are uncomfortable talking about themselves to others without coming across as too shy or too egotistical.

The interview is usually a multiple-step process, not a one-time experience. Many districts require the candidate to interview with several different individuals. Some interviews are conducted by a single school representative, and others are conducted by a team, which may include classroom teachers, curriculum specialists, special teachers, administrators, and even parents.

### Do Your Homework

Before you go for an interview, research the school district. Many districts will provide you with information about the school system. Many local real estate agents in the school district have information about schools for prospective homebuyers and might share it with you, too.

Local libraries also have demographic information about surrounding school districts. Recently, school districts have been creating web sites where they post information about student achievement, curriculum, and staffing. Most state education departments have web sites for each school district. You might also take a drive around the school district to see what the community looks like.

## Tips for a Successful Interview

The following simple tips can reduce your anxiety and help you focus on presenting your qualifications to the interviewer.

### Be Yourself

This statement seems obvious, but many candidates believe they have to put on an act to be hired. If you want to act, join the theater; if you want to teach, be yourself! Your personal happiness depends on finding the right match between your personality, strengths, and skills and the school district. That decision is complex and involves many factors; do not complicate it by not being true to yourself.

### PREPARE, PREPARE, AND PREPARE SOME MORE

The best thing you can do to ensure a successful interview is prepare yourself as well as possible. What does this mean?

*Keep the purpose of the interview in mind.* This exercise helps you organize your thoughts. Then, anticipate the kinds of questions the interviewer will ask during the session, and practice your responses with a friend.

*Review your qualifications.* Recall experiences that support your qualifications for the position, and rehearse answers to practice questions.

*Think of ways to dissipate the stress of the interview.* Sit up straight, breathe deeply and slowly, and smile. Teachers work in a stressful environment in which they are expected to manage student behavior, respond to multiple stimuli, and communicate well. Your composure during the interview reflects how you might handle the stress of your classroom.

## Focus on Knowledge, Skills, and Experiences

The interviewer's main goal is to determine whether you can teach. When you answer questions, provide relevant information that demonstrates you have what it takes to be a good teacher.

If you are asked, "How would you teach reading to a second grade class of at-risk students?" do not respond with "Well, I was student teacher of the year," or "I attended the International Reading Association's state conference and sat in on a workshop about at-risk readers." These answers do not answer the question. Being named student teacher of the year is nice, and attending a conference may be important in acquiring new knowledge and skills, but this information is not relevant to the question. An appropriate response would be, "When I was student teaching, I used _____, which was successful with these second grade at-risk students. Other methods that were successful in the classroom were _____." Responding to specific questions by *citing personal experiences* demonstrates your knowledge and teaching skills.

## Dress Conservatively

Your interview is not a time for colored or spiked hair, outlandish clothing, or a nose ring. Selena Smith, a middle school principal, reported that a recent male applicant for a position in her building (located in a conservative suburban school district) came to the interview wearing a hot pink shirt, loud plaid jacket, and makeup. We could not invent a story like this. Personal preferences in your appearance and style of dress may be appropriate in some settings but rarely are accepted in the mainstream employment world.

The interviewer expects you to be at your best, in terms of both appearance and presentation. Researching the school district can provide you with ideas about how you should dress. Your best bet is to be conservative in terms of clothing, makeup, and accessories. Your credentials will get you the interview, but your interview will get you the job.

## USE PROPER ENGLISH

You make an impression on the interviewer, or committee, during the interview. One of the characteristics of an effective teacher is to be able to communicate well. School districts are under increasing pressure to produce graduates who can read, write, and compute at grade level. Teachers are the key models of effective communication skills for students.

A sure way to end an interview quickly is to butcher the English language. Think through your response before answering the question. If speaking in grammatical English sentences is difficult for you, spend some time before the interview working on your speaking skills. Have friends or family members ask you mock interview questions, and tape your responses. Play them back, listening for errors in grammar—get someone else to listen with you if you need help—and then plan and practice a better answer. That way, you'll be prepared with grammatical answers to many of the questions you might be asked—and that will make you more relaxed and confident when facing the questions you *didn't* anticipate.

## The Interview: What to Expect

Thinking about the interview ahead of time and having an idea what to expect will help quell your anxiety.

### The Questions

Listen carefully, and answer questions directly. Supporting information, such as a short anecdote, adds color and interest to your response and provides clues to the interviewer about what kind of teacher you might be in the classroom. However, do not ramble on, and do not fake answers. If you do not know the answer, just say so. Ask the interviewer to repeat any question that you don't understand.

If you say you are familiar with a program or philosophy of education, then be prepared to answer additional questions about it. Be prepared for open-ended questions such as, "If you were walking and came to a fork in the path and one way led to a lower path and the other led to a less-traveled higher path, which one would you take, and why?" Be prepared to answer difficult questions about yourself and what might affect your performance as a teacher. Some of the following questions are common:

- What are the greatest strengths that you will bring to this position, and how will you compensate for your weaknesses?
- What would you do if you truly believed in involving parents in your classroom, but your colleagues told you not to because it made them look bad?

- How would you construct a lesson on a particular piece of content in your subject area?

You should anticipate at least a few questions at this level of specificity:

- How do you get parents on your side?
- Are you familiar with the content and performance standards for your state?
- What is your philosophy of teaching and learning?
- How do you know what to teach? How do you teach it, and how do you know when students have learned it?
- What will your classroom look like, and why?

You also might be asked hypothetical questions such as, "A parent complains to you at a conference that her child is not reading. What is reading, and how do you teach it?"

You should weave your beliefs, values, and philosophy into the answers. Each answer should portray your level of character, degree of responsibility, and depth of ownership. Overall, the interviewer will evaluate your enthusiasm and emotional maturity.

Interviewers cannot legally ask you questions pertaining to specific aspects of your personal life. These areas include:

- national origin or citizenship
- age
- marital/family status
- affiliations
- personal (physical) characteristics
- disabilities
- arrest record
- military record

There are ways that interviewers can find out such information without asking you these specific questions. For example, whereas the interviewer cannot ask whether you are married or if you have children, the interviewer may ask whether you are able to fulfill after-school responsibilities such as sponsoring a club or coaching a team. You must choose whether to answer or to respectfully decline. Sometimes a casual conversation will lead you into these areas. You must decide in advance how you plan to respond; if you become defensive, the outcome of the interview may be affected.

### Portfolio

The interview is an appropriate time to support your answers using a portfolio. A portfolio is a statement of your teaching qualifications presented in scrapbook format. Some teacher education schools require that you develop a portfolio as a part of your student teaching experience. However, many districts do not consider a portfolio an important component of the interview process.

A portfolio may include, but is not limited to, evaluations from your supervisors and teachers, photographs from student teaching, samples of lessons and units you have developed, and professional letters of reference. Have it organized by section so that you can immediately turn to the section of the portfolio that is needed.

### Your Questions

The interview also is an opportunity for you to ask questions about the position and the school district. Usually, toward the end of the interview, the interviewer will invite you to ask questions. Do not ask off-the-cuff questions. Knowing the school district and the position you are applying for, prepare your questions in advance. Ask questions that will help you decide whether you want to teach in this school district.

Some questions that are usually inappropriate to ask early in the interview process are:

- What is my salary?
- When are vacations?
- Who do I have lunch with?
- When is my conference/preparation time?

Instead, ask questions that your research has suggested about the student body, about relationships with parents, or about the educational philosophy or policies of the administrators or board of education.

If you are given an opportunity to tour a facility and meet staff members, be prepared to ask them, too, about the operation of the school. Some appropriate questions are:

- How many students do you have in your classroom?
- Can you get additional supplies if they are needed?
- What kind of equipment is available for teacher use?

### Writing

Be prepared to provide a sample of your writing to the interviewer. Some districts require that you write an essay on the topic of their choice as part of the interview process. Once you have the topic, carefully organize your thoughts before writing. Writing is an important skill for a teacher. If we expect our students to write well, we must be able to model that process.

## THE DEMONSTRATION LESSON

Many districts require you to develop and teach a demonstration lesson. You may actually teach the lesson to a class of students. Find out how much time you will have, who your audience will be, and the subject or lesson you're expected to teach. If you aren't given specifics, you should have a variety of lesson options (lesson or small group) and a set of lessons or topics you'd be willing to teach. Showing your interviewers or observers that you can offer choices will demonstrate your range and confidence.

You are encouraged to consult with the classroom teacher for guidance in preparing the lesson. How you handle this assignment is a defining part of the interview process. You can get a tremendous amount of help from the classroom teacher. However, information will not be volunteered—you must ask for it. Teacher candidates who show up five minutes before class time with a canned activity will not be as successful as those who take time to carefully prepare a lesson.

The first step is to call the school and speak with the secretary. School secretaries know everything that is going on! Ask when the teacher is available. Some of the questions you should ask are:

- What topic is the class studying?
- What was taught before this lesson?

- What are the children like?
- Do the children have special needs?
- Is this a heterogeneous class?
- Can I bring nametags with me for the children?
- Who will be observing the lesson?
- When can I come in to meet the children?

Your goal is to look like you belong in the class. The more you know about the children and what they have been doing, the more comfortable you all will be. Some candidates spend an entire day in the school, before teaching the lesson, to get a feeling for the students. You are not expected to be perfect, but you are expected to be engaging and connect with the students.

Keep these tips in mind:

- Demonstrate your organization skills. Tell your audience what they'll learn, teach it, and review.
- Show enthusiasm. Draw on your public speaking skills—use eye contact, facial expressions, body language, appropriate humor, and voice modulation.
- The best lessons are often interactive. Ask questions and keep the audience engaged.
- Multimedia can enhance your lesson if used properly. Your goal is for these devices (handouts, music, illustrations, etc.) to illustrate, not detract from, your presentation.
- Practice! You might even record your lesson to evaluate yourself.

The observers are looking for a person who is professional, caring, and knowledgeable. Plan to *teach something new* to the children, based on their needs. Also bring a formal written lesson plan to give to each of the observers.

## THE FOLLOW-UP

It is advisable to follow up with a letter thanking the interviewer for his or her time and consideration during the interview, preferably within 24 hours of the interview. Statistically less than 10% of interviewees follow up with a thank-you letter, so you will be part of the 10% that stands out. The letter assures your continued interest in the position. The letter should briefly reemphasize some of your better qualifications for the position and your interest in the position and be as concise and focused as your cover letter and resume. In addition, a thank-you letter to the classroom teacher is a nice touch, but it should not be a carbon copy of the other thank-you letters. (Remember to ask for business cards before leaving the interview so you have the correct spelling of names and titles for everyone.)

The interview itself is like the big game of the season. All the preceding preparation is for naught if you cannot effectively communicate your qualifications to the interviewer. Take heart, though: By the time you meet your interviewer, you have been well-prepared academically, you have learned from experiences in the classroom, and you have reflectively prepared for the interview. With all of this preparation, you will do fine, so relax!

## THE INSIDE TRACK

| | |
|---|---|
| Who: | Andrea Lupica |
| What: | High School English Teacher |
| Where: | Cliffside Park High School, Cliffside Park, NJ |
| Type of School: | Public |

| | |
|---|---|
| How long: | 4 Years |
| Degree(s): | BA in English Literature & MAT |
| School(s): | Fairleigh Dickinson University |

### Insider Advice

When I first started all of the veteran teachers warned me that it was very important to not smile at the students until at least January. I thought they were exaggerating and that the students would respond well to the warmth of a smile; I was wrong. I learned my lesson the hard way and paid for it by having a horrible first year with very little control of my classes. After that first year I make sure that my students understand that it is my classroom, not theirs, until I feel they have earned an opportunity to share in its claim.

### What I Wish I Had Learned in School

I quickly realized that in college more of the lessons were geared toward those learning to be early education teachers. Many of the examples of tests, lesson plans, and strategies were of grammar school classes. I really wished more time could be given to showing secondary educators how to manage the short periods we have with the students.

### Greatest Joy

The greatest joy I have now is seeing students who have graduated and come to visit me. They always remember some of the greatest classroom experiences that I sometimes forget because there are so many classes to remember. They also come to me asking for help with some of their college workload which makes me happy because it shows that I have earned their trust somewhere along the way.

### Biggest Drawback

Most people think that teachers have it easy because they only work about 180 days a year. Yeah, right! The truth of it is I have never worked harder at any other job. Being a teacher is more like a 365-day-a-year job. Between 8:00 A.M. and 3:00 P.M. I teach in a classroom, and that's the easy part. After 3:00 I grade papers, write exams and worksheets, figure out lesson plans, organize classroom events, plan field trips, and work out all of the other things that come my way as a teacher.

### Future Plans

Teach and learn. I plan to go back to school as soon as possible because teaching can get stale if you don't find a way to rejuvenate it. Being open to new ideas and trying them out in your classroom is the best way to continue to love your job.

# CHAPTER six

## HOW TO SUCCEED ONCE YOU'VE LANDED THE JOB

**NEW TECHNOLOGY** and approaches to teaching are creating many possibilities for educators today. At the same time, today's teachers still face many of the same challenges as teachers in the past—conflicting job expectations, reduced resources, and limited freedom.

You learned many important things in your teacher education program. Still, all the education courses in the world won't help you manage your relationships with other teachers, staff, the principal, and parents. This chapter gives you tips for being successful during your first year on the job.

You got the job you dreamed of and are ready to begin your career. Taking out your education manuals, you start to plan the first lessons. You collect all the teacher's editions and manuals available and read all the students' records in the guidance files. You think you are ready to start, but one major ingredient must be added to the mix: input from senior staff members.

The key to your happiness and high student achievement often depends on your interaction within the school community, that is, your working relationship with your colleagues. Building these relationships is the most important first step to take when starting any new job. Every school has a culture. Your job is to learn this culture and become part of it. Doing this will help you succeed as a teacher and can determine your ultimate success in the classroom.

## FITTING IN

A school is a complete community—self-contained in many ways, yet part of another community, that is, the district that encompasses the building. The school district (the official hiring agency) defines the set of rules and regulations that structure your workday. These regulations often appear in a policy manual and provide specific prescriptions for handling problems, expectations for your teaching day, and general do's and don'ts set by the board of education. In addition, there may be a teacher contract from your union or professional association that explains the specific details of your job. However, the *unwritten code* of behavior within your particular building is what you want to capture before you begin to teach.

### Unwritten Expectations

The time you should arrive at school may be listed in the teacher handbook, in the union contract, or in the board of education policy book. Although the requirements are defined, they do not tell you what really happens. For example, the teacher workday may be listed as seven hours, beginning at 8:20 A.M. Because the children do not arrive at the building until 9:00 A.M., when the buses pull in, this may seem logical to you. On the first day of school, you leave your house expecting to arrive right on time at 8:20 A.M. However, when you get to the school, you find a parking lot completely filled—you are the last one in! Are you on time? Technically, yes. Culturally, for that school, no!

In this particular school, many faculty members come in earlier than required to have breakfast together, socialize, copy materials, or complete professional work assignments. This culture can differ dramatically among schools within a district. It is your job to learn and interpret these small nuances that are part of the school culture. Social arrangements for weekend or after-school gatherings may be made during these times, and you should take part. To belong to a school community, you must have shared experiences that bind you to other staff members and make you part of the culture.

Your first task is to be a good detective and learn who the players are. Listen carefully to the clues presented by colleagues in conversational moments, and learn to ask questions that will help you understand the culture of the school.

## Make Friends with the Secretaries

In your building, several people run the operation. The secretaries are the most visible. Stop in often to say, "Good Morning!" or to see if you can deliver anything to any other staff members for them. Your friendly approach will benefit you over and over again.

The front office is a gathering place for staff members, so the secretaries know all personnel and the staff hierarchy. *Get to know the secretaries!* Learn what they do, because they will point you in the right direction when you need information. They know who is in charge of what curriculum area and how to get what you need for your classroom.

## Listen to Other Teachers and the Administrators

Your colleagues are extremely important to your success. To begin with, they already know the culture of the building because they are not only part of it but also create change as they see necessary. Before you even walk into your classroom, find out who else is in your department or on your grade level. You can ask a secretary or your administrator—a department chairperson, an assistant principal, or whoever your principal has put in charge of your area. If your school is a one-person operation, go to that person: the principal. Never be afraid to ask pertinent questions of your administrators or colleagues.

Most teachers go back to the school sometime in August. Often they have been required to pack everything up at the end of the previous term, so they must set up their rooms again. Particularly for K–4 teachers, this can take up to two weeks. As a new teacher, you will want to set up your own room. If you are replacing a teacher who retired and used the same classroom you will be using, there will probably be cartons for you to sort through. You will also have new supplies to unpack and you will want to set up your own desk in a way that will work best for you. Call your school to find out when you can come in to visit your new colleagues, offer to help them, and set up your own room.

## FIRST-YEAR TEACHER BURNOUT

Nearly half of all teachers quit during their first five years, according to the National Center for Education Statistics. As one teacher confided, "There are real challenges; large class sizes, disciplinary issues, inadequate materials and funding, inadequate support and training, and the administrative pressure to follow mandates and to excel on high-stakes tests. Too much pressure is placed on a teacher in a single year."

Teacher burnout occurs when a teacher cannot perform the day-to-day duties of teaching due to a sense of tiredness, frustration, exhaustion, and/or hopelessness. The teacher either leaves the situation or stays in the same position and, in general, is unsuccessful or ineffective as a teacher. Here are ten tips for avoiding first-year teacher burnout:

1. Create "me time" outside of school.
2. Continue your hobbies or interests during leisure time.
3. Stay positive and surround yourself with positive people.
4. Always use your time wisely.
5. Set priorities, concentrating on what needs to be done for the day.
6. Reward yourself for the good things you did each day and learn from the mistakes.
7. Organize your life in and out of the classroom.
8. Ask lots of questions—remember, there are things you do not know until you ask.
9. Reach out for support both in and out of school.
10. Get plenty of rest, exercise, and eat healthy.

## Consult with Other Professional Staff

Many staff members can help you adjust to the school. Within every setting, there are support personnel who work with your children regularly. Children may have the same art, music, physical education, technology, and library science teachers throughout their elementary school experience. These teachers may have already worked with your students (unless you teach kindergarten) for several years and may have some interesting information to help guide your instruction. They also have specific skills that can assist you in the classroom and enhance your curriculum. These teachers can work with you to integrate the curriculum by supplementing the course of study in art, music, or physical education. The librarian can prepare materials for you and work with your children on a research project. A collegial approach is a healthy way for you to integrate yourself into the staff culture.

Other staff members also work cooperatively with classroom teachers to help selected students. Like the curriculum teachers, many of these teachers and support personnel may already know some of your students. If they are going to work with your students, then you must work with them, too. Be assertive; seek them out, because they can be great sources of information and support to you. Often supplying mandated services to children who need extra help, these include:

- remedial reading teacher
- remedial mathematics teacher
- teacher of the gifted
- resource room teacher
- speech and language teacher
- psychologist
- guidance counselor

The entire school community is your resource, and the more you expand your network to include all staff members, the easier your transition and integration will be.

Take the time to learn who your colleagues are, what their strengths are, and how you can engage them in your personal growth as a teacher. As one teacher confesses, "The teachers with whom I've been on staff were an extremely valuable connection. The colleagues I have met at seminars, classes, and in-service gatherings were also an invaluable source. And although I moved to several different states over the years, I maintained contact with former colleagues." Once you become a part of the process, you, too, will be asked for advice.

## QUESTIONS TO ASK FELLOW TEACHERS

Begin to establish relationships with your colleagues by asking questions. If you get your assignment during the summer before the school year starts, ask the secretaries for home telephone numbers of teachers in your school or department. Do not be afraid to call and introduce yourself.

Some of these questions seem obvious, but the only way to learn what the culture is and how to become part of it is to ask.

- Are the other members of my grade level or department getting together over the summer? Would it be possible for me to attend?
- How do you begin the first day of school?
- What are the procedures the first day and week of school?
- Are these procedures different from the rest of the school year?
- What kinds of materials are used in addition to prescribed textbooks?
- When is planning time?
- How is planning time used? Do grade levels plan curriculum together?
- Can I see a plan book that has been used and spells out the development of the curriculum?
- How do you determine the length of time spent on a unit?
- Is there a common or agreed-upon length of time to spend in each area?
- What time do the teachers arrive at school?
- What time do the teachers go home?
- Do all of the teachers eat together? If not, where do the staff members in my unit or grade level go for lunch?
- How often do you contact parents?
- Is parent contact done by phone or in writing?
- Do you keep records of parent contact?
- Do you meet with every parent who requests a conference?
- How do you record test grades and other marks?
- How do you determine student grades? What constitutes an A, B, C, or D (or whatever marking system is in place)?

- What happens if I fail a student?
- What do you do when you have to be absent? Do you leave specific plans, or is the substitute responsible for carrying on with a general outline?
- Is there a specific substitute my grade level prefers to use?
- Would you mind helping me out with . . . ? (Any number of issues can be filled in here.)

## Be Humble

Fitting in at any new job can be difficult. Don't be ashamed to ask a lot of questions of your fellow teachers and school faculty. Also, be willing to admit you have a lot to learn from experienced teachers. This shows that you are truly committed to being the best possible educator you can be.

Enthusiasm is contagious. A new teacher must take a tremendous amount of time to prepare for lessons, and everything will be easier if you have the friendship, cooperation, and assistance of your colleagues.

If teaching is your second career, you may have spent many years in the business community or in another position in the school system. But in your new job, you're no better off than a new college graduate. Remember that you are the new kid on the block until you prove yourself in the classroom.

One useful tip for fitting in at your new school is to go to the faculty room for lunch. Although it's tempting to stay in your room to get things done, a great deal of sharing goes on during lunchtime, and you can learn a lot. Try to listen to your fellow teachers. When teachers have been there for a while, they know what they are doing. There may be people who think differently than you do, but remember that various methodologies, teaching styles, and personalities suit the various learning styles of the students. You can share what you are doing with the others, but also try to find time to watch the more senior staff members, because they are wise. You must show them you respect what they are doing before you ask them to listen to you.

Your fellow teachers can be a lifeline to you as a new teacher. Some of your colleagues might help your professional development by:

- sharing lesson plans that put curriculum standards into practice
- supporting and participating in your planning process

- offering tips on the practical problems you didn't learn about in school, from limited resources to bureaucracy
- observing your classes or letting you observe their classes
- helping you locate materials

## GETTING TO KNOW THE HIERARCHY

One of the most important keys to your success as a teacher at any level is to be able to get what you need to help the students in your class. You will need supplies, information, cooperation, and assistance from many interested parties. The first person to consider when you need help is your immediate supervisor.

Your immediate supervisor and your principal almost certainly took part in the decision to hire you to teach the specific class you're teaching, and they want you to succeed. So, it is in your best interest to get to know your principal, vice or assistant principal, curriculum supervisor, and director. A hierarchy of supervisors may work with you along the road to success, and each individual will play an important role at some point. Seek them out, and begin a congenial relationship that allows you to have regular conversations with these administrators.

### The Principal's Job

The principal is in charge of the entire building. The ultimate responsibility for everyone and everything comes back to the principal's desk. He or she must answer to the members of the board of education, who make the policies that guide the district; to the superintendent, who is responsible for the achievement in all schools within a district; and to the parents and guardians of every student in the school community. Your job as a teacher is to provide the best educational opportunities and instruction for each and every one of your students. For your principal to succeed, he or she must provide you with the guidance and materials that allow you to do that. There may be an intermediary supervisor between you and the principal, but your principal is nevertheless informed.

The principal monitors attendance (including yours), enrollment, hiring and placement of all kinds of personnel, and custodial and transportation issues; prepares budgets; orders supplies; implements curriculum; conducts after-school activities; and works with parent groups. If you have any questions about the school, the principal will advise you, point you in the right direction to find an answer, or otherwise help you handle a problem.

## The Principal as Problem Solver

Some people try to avoid letting their supervisor know when something has gone wrong. They may be embarrassed and try to fix it themselves. This approach is disastrous for a teacher. It usually makes things worse, rather than better, and complicates the situation.

Keep your principal informed. As a new teacher, you do not have the background or experience to make informed decisions about difficult situations. Your colleagues may be able to help guide you through a specially requested parent or guardian conference, for example, but your principal has a long-term history of decision making and should be the first person you go to for advice.

### How to Handle a Parent or Guardian Problem

Parents and guardians may request to see you because they are concerned about their child's progress. They may claim, "You are not challenging my child." (Don't be offended, but parents and guardians sometimes request not to have a beginning teacher, because they fear that your inexperience will have a negative effect on their child's instruction.)

Your principal has weathered situations like this before. He or she may know these parents or guardians well, having heard the same complaint from them before. The principal can help you plan the conference and perhaps suggest words you can use to calm down the parents or guardians. If you plan ahead, you are more likely to have the parents on your side by the end of the meeting.

Meet with your principal again after the conference. The principal will respect your careful handling of the situation; he or she would much rather counsel you ahead of time than have to clean up an unpleasant situation afterward.

### How Not to Handle a Parent or Guardian Problem

Picture the same example handled another way: You arrange the conference yourself; the parents or guardians are unimpressed with the outcome and go straight to your principal. The principal is caught off guard, cannot respond to the parents or guardians immediately (because he or she does not have the information needed to make a judgment), and can only temporarily calm the waters. The parents or guardians are angry or frustrated; the principal has to arrange to meet with you to find out what happened and why, and *then* plan another meeting with the parents or guardians to resolve the problem.

What could have been one preliminary meeting between you and the principal has instead turned into three or four stressful interactions involving you and the parents or guardians. "Why didn't you come to me first?" is the question any principal would ask. The principal will not question your judgment if you ask, "How should I handle this?" or "Do you have any suggestions or information to help me with this conference?" Your judgment will be questioned, however, if you continue to operate in a manner that causes your administrator extra stress.

### The Principal Versus Everyone Else

All the advice you get may not be good. One teacher may say, "Everyone does it this way," yet you truly believe that another method would be more comfortable for you. Talk with your principal or immediate supervisor about it. The administration may have actively sought a teacher who could take a stand and use a new technique or method.

Reading, for example, was taught for many years with a *basal approach*. Students read together from a basal reader, completed exercises in phonics and practice books, and worked only with students on a similar reading level. Several years ago, a new philosophy called *whole language* was introduced. This method was different in that teachers worked from complete novels, with students of varying ability, and connected the reading exercise to a writing assignment. Teachers using this instructional pattern required knowledge of whole-language strategies and an understanding of how to assess student progress with these methods.

You may have been hired because you have training in a technique that the principal wants introduced into the curriculum. Other teachers may be doing things differently, but that is irrelevant. Find out what the principal wants. Change within a school is often needed but hard to do. One way for a principal to make it happen is to hire candidates who demonstrate interest or proficiency in the needed area. If you are questioned or even confronted, you must let people know that you have the support of the administration.

It also is important that you never compromise your belief in a child. You are his or her advocate for that year, and you must follow through and follow up on that child's behalf. If you are unhappy about how one of your students was spoken to or reprimanded, handle it carefully with the other staff member, but handle it. You must speak out, even if you are new. Your principal can suggest words to diplomatically keep your colleagues engaged while continuing to implement your project, program, or philosophy.

## BEING OBSERVED

Your supervisors will want to watch you work in the classroom. Formal observations are expected several times each year. These lessons are sometimes carefully planned, and teachers may use "bells and whistles" to impress the supervisors. Supervisors know this happens, but they want to see *the real you*. Informal pop-ins on your class and spontaneous conversations with you provide that insight.

During a class observation, your supervisor will scan your classroom and note the answers to the following questions:

- Does the classroom reflect the students' work?
- How does the teacher manage discipline?
- What systems or routines does the teacher have in place that demonstrate his or her guidelines for student performance?
- How do students interact with each other when they are with the teacher?
- Are students organized in a variety of grouping structures (whole, small, cooperative, partners) to meet high, middle, and low achievers' needs?
- How does the teacher speak to the students?
- Does the teacher listen to the students?
- Are the plans listed in the teacher's plan book being implemented?
- What materials is the teacher using?
- Are the teacher's instructional strategies varied and appropriate for the students?

- Does the teacher provide for higher level questioning, sufficient wait time for student responses, and positive feedback to student responses?
- Does the teacher provide summary or closure at the end of the lesson to review the objective and reinforce what was taught and learned?
- Is the room organized?
- Is the classroom atmosphere warm, caring, and nurturing?
- Is the room clean?
- Is active learning going on?
- Is the room safe?

Some of these items may seem silly to you, but the answers tell a story about you and your students. They indicate who you are and how you work. The better your supervisor knows you, the better you will be supported when you ask for supplies or assistance.

## FINDING A MENTOR

You're most likely familiar with the phrase "sink or swim." As the start of your first school year approaches, anxiety may be increasing as you picture yourself dropped into a challenging situation—difficult classrooms, quick orientation on school policies and procedures, confusion over school curriculum—with little preparation or help. Enter the teacher mentor.

As a beginning teacher, you often will need someone to turn to for immediate answers. Who should you approach, and who should you trust? Your administrator can point you in the right direction and help you find positive role models who are doing a good job and are successful in the classroom. Asking for help in identifying a mentor can only enhance your performance, and it helps you establish a relationship with the administration—especially if you follow their suggestions. Once you are in the building for a while, you can add to that cadre of advisors.

Increasingly, many districts are working with teacher associations or universities to establish mentoring programs for new teachers, veteran teachers in new assignments, and teachers in need of remedial aid. Experienced teachers are paid a stipend to assist the newest faculty members, and time is set aside to plan and to review specific lessons and general plans. More than half the states now require teacher mentors for new teachers. In Missouri, for instance, this support system is mandated by law; individual districts also may formalize such a plan. The teachers selected to be mentors have been judged by administrators to be outstanding teachers. In other districts, retired teachers are hired to observe the classrooms of the new teachers and to assist in the development of lessons, instructional groups, and behavior modification programs. Again, master teachers are worth listening to.

When you feel established in the school and have gotten to know your colleagues, you'll be in a better position to choose your own mentor. To start, work with whomever your principal recommends or your district assigns. You need someone who can give you answers when you need them. If your assigned mentor isn't a perfect fit, look for someone whose style or personality better matches your own after you become more established.

## MAKING THE MOST OF YOUR UNION

In the United States, there are two major national unions that work with teachers to assist and guide them during their career and sometimes into retirement: the American Federation of Teachers (AFT) and the National Education Association (NEA). Membership in one of these associations can be useful in your career.

### How the Union Works

You may have very little contact with the national level of AFT or NEA; the local or state affiliate affects your daily life much more than the national organization. If you decide to join a union, you join the "local," just like any other union worker. Each local association gets information and advice from the state and national levels of the organization.

In some school districts, both organizations are represented in one school. In that case, each teacher chooses whether to join one or the other or neither. In other districts, only one of these two organizations is represented on the staff. Some districts are "union shops," which means that every teacher hired must join the organization. In that case, dues are deducted automatically from your paycheck, and you become a union member as soon as you become a staff member. Some districts may not belong to a national organization but have one or two state and local groups that provide a service for you.

Whether the AFT or the NEA dominates and whether you are under obligation to join varies within districts, counties, and states. When you have a choice of organizations to join, find out the benefits of each. If everyone in your building belongs to one organization, though, it is smart to go with the crowd. You do not want to stand alone on issues, and differences may arise later that you cannot predict now. You will jeopardize your ability to fit in to the culture if you are the solitary member of a national teacher organization in your building—or if you are the solitary non-union member.

## What the Union Does for You

In some districts, one organization negotiates and handles your contract. Elected officials such as a president and vice president represent your interests and the interests of all the teachers in the school community. The local officials bargain for a contract and work with the board of education to determine your salary, health insurance benefits, and working conditions.

## Working with Union Representatives

Local union representatives may be valuable sources of advice. After all, they were elected by the other faculty; they must be respected by their peers. They often are knowledgeable senior staff members who can help you answer questions and handle problems that arise when dealing with issues within your school and district. They can help you navigate the maze of confusion that comes with being a new teacher. Unions are very helpful and provide information and assistance about some of the following areas:

- opportunities for professional growth
- your retirement system
- your health plan and/or options
- group insurance for your household
- legal assistance (at a group rate)

- understanding your contract (if you are bound by one)
- filing papers to go on leave or retire
- opportunities to purchase at a discount
- solving problems in a large bureaucratic system

Unions are designed to assist you and enhance your well-being. It is up to you to make the most of the opportunities they offer.

## WHAT YOU WISH YOU'D LEARNED IN SCHOOL

You may become frustrated because situations keep arising in class that were not discussed in school. A principal or any other supervisor who has been a classroom teacher knows that it takes many years to become a *master teacher*. A master teacher starts to build a portfolio of ideas as the years progress. These experiences form the basis for making decisions about instruction, curriculum, students, parents and guardians, and staff members. Unfortunately, there is no quick and easy way to amass the knowledge and skills that seem to come automatically to experienced teachers. If there were, you would have learned them in your teacher education program.

### TOP FIVE MOVIES ABOUT TEACHING

On the shelves of your local video store or online movie rental website, you can find a number of movies showcasing the true-life stories of remarkable teachers. Check out these inspiring movies based on real teachers:

- *Freedom Writers* (2007)
- *Dangerous Minds* (1995)
- *Dead Poet's Society* (1989)
- *Lean on Me* (1989)
- *Stand and Deliver* (1988)

## BECOME A LIFETIME LEARNER

You took classes, got firsthand experience, and spent time and money preparing for your profession. You learned many things in school, but once you start to teach, you discover that there are many things yet to learn. Some are incorporated into your routines by watching and learning from your supervisors, colleagues, and senior staff. Other ideas are found in teacher journals. But that is not enough.

A teacher's professional growth must be continuous, so it is expected that you attend formal workshops and courses to maintain certification. In fact, many states require a master's degree for permanent certification.

New teachers spend quite a bit of time preparing for the day. Many are in the buildings at 7:00 A.M., preparing lessons and materials, and stay until early evening. It may be hard to summon up the energy to take courses, pay attention, and bring what you learn back into the classroom. But the good news is that when a district offers courses, there is no fee. College courses often cost several hundred dollars per credit, and courses are three credits! They are an expensive way to maintain your professional growth. Districts sometimes join forces with neighboring communities and share staff development services. They bring in some of the best instructors and presenters available. Often, master teachers run the in-service courses, providing an opportunity for you to meet and work with these experts in concentrated curriculum areas.

Sometimes, staff development funds are set aside—within the building or the district—to provide teachers with an opportunity to select and pursue topics of interest. Flyers advertising one- to three-day workshops are sent to schools, often posted on a staff bulletin board or in the faculty room. You have to take the initiative to find out who is in charge of distributing the money and how to apply for these sessions, but opportunities are available.

During the summer, districts often offer one-week courses in a technique or skill that staff members need. Every district is accountable for student achievement, and this success depends on staff training. Because many states are currently implementing new state standards to improve student performance, many districts are offering courses to help staff members learn how to implement the plans. Such courses include instructional techniques and strategies for classroom management.

The U.S. economic recession has limited some state and district education budgets, so good alternatives for those seeking professional development in those regions are professional development grants. There are thousands of grant possibilities that you can find online. Grant-funded education opportunities can allow you to travel the world, pursue your love of learning, and earn elective and required professional development hours.

## PROFESSIONAL DEVELOPMENT WEBSITES

During hard economic times, it is still possible to find free or low-cost curriculum and professional teaching resources. Try the following websites:

### Wiki-Teacher

www.wiki-teacher.com/index.php

This is a valuable source of K–8 lessons and unit plans, which are searchable by keyword, grade-level standard, or a specific textbook. Videos show actual teachers demonstrating their instructional, management, and organizational techniques.

### Teach-nology

www.teach-nology.com/

Here you'll discover 28,000 free K–12 lesson plans, teaching tips, printable worksheets, and games for all subjects. By paying a yearly membership fee, you'll have access to more extensive resources.

### Curriki

http://www.curriki.org/

With this website, you can search through math, science, language arts, or social studies lesson plans and activities for all grade levels. By creating your own user profile, you'll also be able to write blog entries and keep a record of your favorite resources.

### VoyagerU

http://www.voyagerlearning.com/

This website, which specializes in K–12 reading, provides a mixture of group-study sessions with a trained facilitator and individual online activities and assessments. You'll also have access to a variety of lesson plans and activities, such as printable, leveled reading books. Although this website has a substantial fee for its resources, federal School Improvement Funds may cover the costs, and the website itself offers help in finding funding.

### Annenberg Media

http://www.learner.org/

This website offers workshops for K–12 teachers in the arts, foreign language, literature, mathematics, science, and social studies. You can participate in the workshops independently or as part of a group, and have the option of using the hours for graduate credit. You will also find free educational videos that can be downloaded and shown to classes.

### Library of Congress—Teachers Page

http://www.loc.gov/teachers/

Here, you can find ideas for teaching with primary sources; explore an online resource providing free access to photographs, sound recordings, and historical writings that document the American experience; and view grade 4–12 lesson plans and activities in history, government, and literature.

## MANAGING PARENT AND GUARDIAN RELATIONSHIPS

When you are hired to work with students, there is an *unwritten* agreement that you will also work with their parents or guardians and other community members. Parents and guardians trust that the schools will do the right thing for their children, and it is your job to keep them informed about school achievement.

## THE FIRST MEETING

The first time you meet the parents or guardians of your students is very important, because they want to know who you are. They want to be sure that you know what you are doing and that their child will flourish with you.

At the beginning of the school year, you may want to prepare a letter introducing yourself to your students and their parents or guardians. It does not have to be lengthy, but it should include your role in the classroom and your educational background, and it should stress your appreciation and availability to students and parents.

Many districts have a Back-to-School-Night or Meet-the-Teacher-Night at the beginning of the school year. You have a limited time, with a large group of parents and guardians, to present yourself positively and professionally. Middle schools and high schools often ask parents and guardians to follow a student schedule, and you will have only ten to fifteen minutes to get your message across to each group. Elementary teachers may get up to an hour to present the curriculum to their audience. In either scenario, you must be positive and clear. At these events teachers usually do not devote time to individual parent concerns. If parents or guardians confront you with questions that are inappropriate, thank them for their interest and invite them to schedule an appointment with you. If you are flustered or angered by a question, maintain your composure, smile, and say, "We can discuss that privately." Stay in control, and never let them see you sweat!

## TIPS FOR BACK-TO-SCHOOL NIGHT

1. Prepare any materials you wish to distribute, organize your room, and prepare your notes in advance.

2. Begin by welcoming everyone and thanking them for coming. Then, make sure to give a brief description about yourself (education, teaching experience, and interests).

3. Stay positive and use humor.

4. Map out your typical school day, giving times and days for extra activities (if applicable) such as art, music, and physical education.

5. Communicate your homework policy, specifically the amount, frequency, grading, and any student resources available.

6. Explain your overall grading system.

7. Review any discipline procedures in the school and within your classroom.

8. Provide a schedule for parents and guardians indicating times when they can reach you and your contact information (telephone and/or e-mail).

## Report Cards

Another way you interact with parents and guardians is through report cards, which formally present student achievement in an organized format. Your job is to get the message across clearly and concisely. Entire books have been written to help you write and organize comments. Some parents and guardians just look for grades; others want to read the supporting commentary with it.

First and foremost, find something positive to say about each child. You want the parent on your side. If the child is not doing well, you must convey that message to the parent, but you want the parent to work with you, not against you. Comments such as, "He doesn't do his work, and when it's done, it is sloppy" will not yield the cooperation you need from the parent. This comment should be rephrased to, "John seems to have a difficult time completing assignments. I have confidence he is capable of doing the work, and if he slows down, his work will be neater and more organized." This comment says basically the same thing but sends a very different message. It shows that you see positive attributes in the child and that you are confident that the child can improve and grow. It also lets the parents or guardians know that their child is not completing the work and is messy about it! Taking the time to carefully compose your comments will save you time later.

## Keep the Lines of Communication Open

Being accessible to parents and guardians makes it easier for them to be accountable for student performance *with* you, as your partner. Problems are prevented when small issues are addressed at the outset, before they become big issues. If they are not addressed early on, the parent-teacher relationship can become adversarial, rather than collegial, which can interfere with the student's progress.

Parents and guardians' expectations are not always clearly communicated to their children's teachers. They want to trust the teacher, and they want the teacher to be responsive to their child's individual needs.

Lara Monaco, mother of a kindergarten student, explains, "I think it's vital that communication is a two-way street. The teacher should know what's going on at home. If my son is off schedule for whatever reason, its valuable information and will help explain his behavior within the classroom. Likewise, I want to know what is going on during the school day, so my husband and I can facilitate his learning outside of the classroom."

## INVOLVING PARENTS AND GUARDIANS: WHEN AND HOW?

The report card should not be the first time a parent hears from you. You have many opportunities to send messages and to interact with them early in the school year. Here are some suggestions.

- Begin early! Send a letter home to both the parent and the child before school begins. Tell them what the school year will be like and what your expectations are. Children *love* to receive mail, and it sets a very positive tone for interactions with the parents and guardians.

- Send home a weekly or monthly newsletter to let parents and guardians know what is going on in the classroom.

- Create a web page that provides information on current class events, personal information, and curriculum being studied in the classroom.

- Invite parents and guardians for a special event such as a science demonstration, a reenactment of a Shakespearean play, or a poetry reading.

- Ask parents and guardians to sign work that is sent home. Leave a space for them to write any comments or concerns they have.

- Call parents and guardians to let them know that students are doing well.

- Call parents and guardians to let them know that students are not completing work as expected.

- Attend PTA meetings or school events to interact with parents and guardians informally.

- Tell parents and guardians when they can reach you at work if they want to contact you.

## Parent Groups

Your school probably has a parent association—sometimes called PTA (Parent Teacher Association), PTO (Parent Teacher Organization), or PTSA (Parent Teacher Student Association). These organizations run functions that raise funds that go back to the school in some form. Materials may be purchased for classroom use, or assembly programs may be brought in for entire grade levels. It is to your benefit to attend and participate in these activities. It sends a message to the parents and guardians that you are part of their community, and they appreciate your presence.

## THE BOARD OF EDUCATION

An important community group to know about is the local board of education. The members are volunteers who are elected by the community to set school policy. You probably do not see them on a regular basis, but you may be invited to speak at a meeting or host them in your school. They may have even been part of your interview committee. They are the ones who actually vote yes or no to hire you after the superintendent recommends you for the position. These people often are the eyes and ears of the community and will know quite a bit about what goes on in individual classrooms.

The trustees of the board of education are only residents when you see them in the community; they become an official governing body only when they are in session. When you approach individuals with personal problems, you are putting them on the spot. It is not fair to treat them that way.

## THE PAYOFF

The first few years of teaching are difficult because you spend endless hours planning lessons, preparing for class, and trying to fit in with your colleagues. Is it worth it? Rewards come at the most unexpected times. One day, a fifth-grade special education teacher unexpectedly received a bouquet of flowers and this note:

Dear Mrs. Jack,

Yesterday, my son Max read to me from a book and I was overwhelmed by his newly acquired ability to read. I just want to say thank you. Your teaching skills have absolutely made a difference in my son's life.

God Bless you!

The entire school cheered for the success of this learning-disabled child who had struggled for so long, and his mother's letter brought smiles to everyone on the staff. This kind of recognition reminds all teachers why we work so hard and why we continue to put forth extra effort and endless time.

Teaching is a profession for the bright, the energetic, and the caring. It's a surefire way to have a rewarding and enriching professional career.

### THE INSIDE TRACK

| | |
|---|---|
| Who: | Stephanie Tramontozzi |
| What: | Basic Art, Portfolio Development, and Fashion Illustration |
| Where: | New Utrecht High School, Frederick Douglas Academy VII, Brooklyn, NY |
| Type of School: | High School |
| | |
| How long: | 8 Years |
| How much: | $55,000 |
| Degree(s): | BFA, Painting; MA, Art and Design Education |
| School(s): | SUNY Purchase, Pratt Institute |

### Insider Advice

You should know what you are getting into when considering education as a career. Vacations, benefits, and the idea that you are doing a good deed for society look great on paper but it takes a certain personality to juggle the tasks and the different levels of stress that come with the job, and the amount of patience and sensitivity needed to deal with children. You will have many rewarding moments but also disappointments. They are both part of the job. It is important to accept both at the end of the day and still know the value of your work.

It is important that you have experience in working with children beforehand. I was lucky that I had taught weekly art lessons in classrooms and studios in addition to my student teaching experience. It really helps in knowing if this is the right career path for you.

### What I Wish I Had Learned in School

I loved the Art and Design Education program at Pratt Institute. We talked about the mind's development through a tactile experience, pedagogical theories and philosophers, artists, art history, our own techniques and mediums as artists, how they can be introduced to children and beginners, and how to allow our students the freedom to make a lesson their own and use it to delve into their own selves make new discoveries. As enjoyable and valuable as these discussions were they excluded some other topics I would have not only found valuable but also essential. I wish that they talked more about ways to hold on to the freedom we wanted to give our students while still having an atmosphere of respect, safety and order. I often dreaded hearing the words "classroom management" when talking about art education. I disliked these words because I thought of them as synonymous with "silent classroom," which I didn't always find to be necessary or productive during my lessons. I felt there were times to be quiet and times when talk and laughter were acceptable and even contributed to a healthy learning experience. I wish that I had a little guidance on how to keep that balance of structure and freedom. Knowing now what I didn't know then, I believe that a whole class could have been devoted to conflict resolution. I can't think of anything more important to developing a classroom atmosphere where students feel safe to express themselves and be equally respectful of their peers.

### Greatest Joy

I loved putting up bulletin boards. Other teachers might tell you how much they begrudge the chore of putting up bulletin boards. They might say they could be spending that valuable time on lesson planning, grading, or tutoring students who need extra help. While this may be true, I took to arranging my bulletin board as one savoring a personal indulgence. I felt like all the strifes and struggles melted away as work was carefully selected and mounted on this small, rectangular exhibition space. I have often thought that this must be unique to an art teacher. This was my way of stepping back and seeing the end result of my lesson. The neatly framed and carefully chosen works would always remind me of the best aspects of being in a classroom. In each work I could remember valuable questions that arose and see struggles in concept and technique overcome. Most importantly, I felt like I had learned something new about each student after they had completed their work and that the work was a profound reminder of their greater potential.

### Biggest Drawback

I did have many disappointments in teaching as well as rewards. I felt that my time and efforts were spread thin while trying to bring many students back to class. It was very hard to balance the time-consuming task of caring for them as individuals—which included writing progress reports (sometimes weekly), letters to parents, phone calls, meetings with parents and counselors, and individual and group tutoring—with the work involved in creating a truly meaningful classroom experience for all the students, particularly the ones that were already giving me their best efforts. Too often I received little to no response for these efforts. I often would see students for the potential they had, believe they were making progress, and then have them disappear from my class. That disappointment was hard to accept.

### Future Plans

I have never been one to believe that I had a life vocation but rather a life full of endeavors that reflect my various interests. This would mean classroom teaching was always finite in my mind. However my focus on the role that art plays in the development of society is a constant. In fact, it plays a large role in my decision-making and career endeavors. Having taught in inner city classrooms has been invaluable to my understanding of individuals, as well as society as a whole. It has also helped in better understanding the role that art plays in my own life. I think that a future endeavor I would like to embark on is to curate art exhibitions for students and emerging artists.

# Appendix A

## Professional Associations

**PROFESSIONAL ASSOCIATIONS** are an essential resource in any field and membership in a professional association is expected in most professions. For teachers, professional associations can provide pathways for continued professional development, training, innovative teaching techniques, and networking with peers and potential employers.

National and state level associations exist for every area of instruction to satisfy teachers' professional needs. This directory helps you locate the general teaching associations as well as organizations for your specialty or specialties that can help you be the best teacher you can be. The organizations listed in this directory provide information related to the teaching profession in general or specifically to your certification or concentration.

### American Association for Employment in Education

aaee.org

e-mail: execdir@aaee.org

3040 Riverside Drive, Suite 125

Columbus OH 43221-2550

Phone: 614-485-1111

### American Alliance for Health, Physical Education, Recreation, and Dance (AAHPERD)

aahperd.org

1900 Association Drive

Reston, VA 20191-1598

Phone: 703-476-3400

800-213-7193

### American Association for Health Education (AAHE)

aahperd.org/AAHE

1900 Association Drive

Reston, VA 20191-1598

Phone: 703-476-3400

800-213-7193

### American Association of Physics Teachers (AAPT)

aapt.org

1 Physics Ellipse

College Park, MD 20740-3845

Phone: 301-209-3311

### American Association of Teachers of French (AATF)

frenchteachers.org

e-mail: abrate@siu.edu

National Headquarters

Mailcode 4510

Southern Illinois University

Carbondale, IL 62901

Phone: 618-453-5733

### American Council on the Teaching of Foreign Languages (ACTFL)

actfl.org

e-mail: headquarters@actfl.org

1001 N. Fairfax Street, Suite 200

Alexandria, VA 22314

Phone: 703-894-2900

## American Federation of Teachers (AFT)

aft.org

555 New Jersey Avenue, NW

Washington, DC 20001

Phone: 202-879-4400

## American String Teachers Association (ASTA)

astaweb.com

e-mail: asta@astaweb.com

4153 Chain Bridge Road

Fairfax, VA 22030

Phone: 703-279-2113

## Association for Career and Technical Education (ACTE)

acteonline.org

1410 King Street

Alexandria, VA 22314

800-826-9972

## Association for Childhood Education International (ACEI)

acei.org

e-mail: headquarters@acei.org

17904 Georgia Avenue, Suite 215

Olney, MD 20832

301-570-2111

Phone: 800-423-3563

## Association for Educational Communications and Technology (AECT)

aect@org

e-mail: aect@aect.org

1800 N. Stonelake Drive, Suite 2

Bloomington, IN 47404

Phone: 877-677-AECT

812-335-7675

### Association for Supervision and Curriculum Development (ASCD)

ascd.org

1703 N. Beauregard Street

1250 Pitt Street

Alexandria, VA 22311-1714

Phone: 800-933-2723

### Association of Teacher Educators (ATE)

ate1.org

P.O. Box 793

Manassas, VA 20113

Phone: 703-331-0911

### Association of Teachers of Spanish and Portuguese (AATSP)

aatsp.org

900 Ladd Road

Walled Lake, MI 48390

Phone: 248-960-2180

### Business Professionals of America (BPA)

bpa.org

5454 Cleveland Avenue

Columbus, OH 43231-4021

Phone: 614-895-7277

### Council for Economic Education

councilforeconed.org

e-mail: customerservice@councilforeconed.org

122 East 42 Street, Suite 2600

New York, NY 10168

Phone: 800-338-1192

### Council for Exceptional Children (Special Education) (CEC)

cec.sped.org

1110 North Glebe Road, Suite 300

Arlington, VA 22201

Phone: 888-232-7733

## Future Business Leaders of America-Phi Beta Lambda, Inc.

fbla-pbl.org

1912 Association Drive

Reston, VA 22091-1591

Phone: 800-325-2946

## International Reading Association (IRA)

reading.org

P.O. Box 8139

800 Barksdale Road

Newark, DE 19714-8139

Phone: 800-336-7323

## International Society for Music Education (ISME)

isme.org

e-mail: isme@isme.org

International Office

P.O. Box 909

Nedlands, WA 6909

Australia

Phone: +61 8 9386 2654

## Music Educators National Conference (MENC)

menc.org

1806 Robert Fulton Drive

Reston, VA 20191

Phone: 703-860-4000

800-336-3768

## National Art Education Association (NAEA)

naea-reston.org

e-mail: Info@ArtEducators.org

1916 Association Drive

Reston, VA 20191-1590

Phone: 703-860-8000

### National Association for Bilingual Education (NABE)

nabe.org

1313 L Street NW, Suite 210

Washington, DC 20005-4100

Phone: 202-898-1829

### National Association for Gifted Children (NAGC)

nagc.org

e-mail: nagc@nagc.org

1707 L Street, NW, Suite 550

Washington, DC 20036

Phone: 202-785-4268

### National Association for Sports and Physical Education (NASPE)

http://www.aahperd.org/Naspe/

1900 Association Drive

Reston, VA 20191-1598

Phone: 703-476-3400

### National Association of Biology Teachers (NABT)

nabt.org

e-mail: office@nabt.org

12030 Sunrise Valley Drive, Suite 110

Reston, VA, 20191-3409

Phone: 703-264-9696

### The National Board for Professional Teaching Standards

nbpts.org

Arlington Office

1525 Wilson Boulevard, Suite 500

Arlington, VA 22209

Phone: 800-22-TEACH

### National Business Education Association

www.nbea.org

1914 Association Drive

Reston, VA 20191

Phone: 703-860-8300

## National Business Education Association (NBEA)

nbea.org

e-mail: nbea@nbea.org

1914 Association Drive

Reston, VA 20191

Phone: 703-860-8300

## National Catholic Education Association (NCEA)

ncea.org

1077 30th Street, NW, Suite 100

Washington, DC 20007-3852

Phone: 800-711-6232

## National Child Care Association (NCCA)

nccanet.org

1325 G Street, NW, Suite 500

Washington, DC 20005

Phone: 800-543-7161

## National Clearinghouse for English Language Acquisition and Language Instruction Educational Programs

ncela.gwu.edu

e-mail: askncela@gwu.edu

2011 Eye Street NW, Suite 300

Washington, DC 20006

Phone: 202-467-0867

## National Commission on Teaching and America's Future (NCTAF)

Teachers College, Columbia University

nctaf.org

e-mail: rbrookshire@nctaf.org

2100 M Street NW, Suite 660

Washington, DC 20037

Phone: 202-429-2570

### National Council for the Social Studies (NCSS)

socialstudies.org

8555 Sixteenth Street, Suite 500

Silver Spring, MD 20910

Phone: 301-588-1800

### National Council of Teachers of English (NCTE)

ncte.org

1111 W. Kenyon Road

Urbana, IL 61801-1096

Phone: 217-328-3870

### National Council of Teachers of Mathematics (NCTM)

nctm.org

e-mail: nctm@nctm.org

1906 Association Drive

Reston, VA 22091-1502

Phone: 703-620-9840

### National Education Association (NEA)

nea.org

1201 16th Street, NW

Washington, DC 20036-3290

Phone: 202-833-4000

### National Middle School Association (NMSA)

nmsa.org

NMSA Headquarters

4151 Executive Parkway, Suite 300

Westerville, OH 43081

Phone: 800-528-NMSA

## National Science Teachers Association (NSTA)

nsta.org

e-mail: membership@nsta.org

1840 Wilson Boulevard

Arlington, VA 22201-3000

Phone: 703-243-7100

## Phi Delta Kappa

pdkintl.org

e-mail: customerservice@ pdkintl.org

408 N. Union Street

Bloomington, IN 47405-3800

Phone: 812-339-1156

## SkillsUSA

skillsusa.org

P.O. Box 3000

Leesburg, VA 20177-0300

Phone: 703-777-8810

Fax: 703-777-8999

## Teachers of English to Speakers of Other Languages (TESOL)

tesol.org

e-mail: info@tesol.org

700 South Washington Street, Suite 200

Alexandria, VA 22314

Phone: 703-836-0774

# Appendix B

## Additional Resources

**YOU KNOW** the basics. Now you need to delve deeper and get the details that will help you get the job done. This directory points you in the right direction to find the information you need to achieve your educational and career goals.

### SUGGESTED LEARNINGEXPRESS BOOKS

#### Test Preparation

411 SAT Algebra & Geometry Questions

411 SAT Critical Reading Questions

411 SAT Writing Questions and Essay Prompts

Acing the GRE

ACT Essay Practice

ACT Preparation in a Flash

Goof-Proof College Admission Essays

GRE Test Prep, 2nd Edition

GRE Test Success in Only 5 Steps!

SAT Writing Essentials

### Teacher Certification

*CBEST: California Basic Skills Test, 4th Edition*

*NYSTCE*

*Praxis I, 3rd Edition SAT Math Essentials*

*Test-Taking Power Strategies*

*TExES*

### Job Search

*Goof-Proof Interviews*

*Goof-Proof Resumes and Cover Letters*

*Job Interviews That Get You Hired*

*Resumes That Get You Hired*

## ONLINE RESOURCES

### College Search

College Board. http://www.collegeboard.com/

CollegeView. http://www.collegeview.com

Education Week. http://www.edweek.org

U.S. Department of Education. http://www.ed.gov/index.jhtml

### Financial Aid

*Free Application for Federal Student Aid.* http://www.fafsa.ed.gov

*Scholarships: On the net.* http://www.advocacy-net.com/scholarmks.htm

*TheSmartStudent™ Guide to Financial Aid.* http://www.finaid.org/

# Appendix C

## Sample Free Application for Federal Student Aid (FAFSA)

**ON THE** following pages, you'll find a sample of the electronic FAFSA, which is faster and often easier than the traditional paper FAFSA. Use this sample to familiarize yourself with the form so that when you apply for federal and state student grants, work-study, and loans you will know what information you need to have ready. When this book went to print, this was the most current version of the form. Although the form remains mostly the same from year to year, you should check the FAFSA website (www.fafsa.ed.gov) for the most current information. Also use this website to learn about application deadlines, school codes, or the status of a submitted FAFSA.

**2009–2010**
FAFSA ON THE WEB WORKSHEET
**www.fafsa.ed.gov**

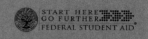

# DO NOT MAIL THIS WORKSHEET.

You must complete and submit a *Free Application for Federal Student Aid* (FAFSA) to apply for federal student aid and to apply for most state and college aid. Applying online with *FAFSA on the Web* at **www.fafsa.ed.gov** is faster and easier than using a paper FAFSA.

For state or college aid, the deadline may be as early as January 2009. See the table to the right for state deadlines. Check with your high school counselor or your college's financial aid administrator about other deadlines.

- **This Worksheet is optional and should only be completed if you plan to use *FAFSA on the Web*.**

- Sections in gray are for parent information.

- In parentheses after each question is the number that is used on *FAFSA on the Web* and the paper FAFSA. However, not all of the questions appear on this worksheet.

- **Submit your FAFSA early, but not before January 1, 2009.**

**Apply Faster—Sign your FAFSA with a Federal Student Aid PIN.**
If you do not have a PIN, you can apply for one at **www.pin.ed.gov**. Your PIN allows you to electronically sign when you submit your FAFSA. If you are providing parent information, one parent must also sign your FAFSA. To sign electronically, your parent should also apply for a PIN.

## You will need the following information to complete this Worksheet:

❑ Your Social Security Number and your parents' Social Security Numbers if you are providing parental information.

❑ Your driver's license number if you have one.

❑ Your Alien Registration Number if you are not a U.S. citizen.

❑ 2008 federal tax information or tax returns (including IRS W-2 information) for yourself (and spouse if you are married) and for your parents if you are providing parental information. If you have not yet filed a 2008 income tax return, you can still submit your FAFSA but you must provide income and tax information.

❑ Information on savings, investments, and business and farm assets for yourself and your parents if you are providing parental information.

| WARNING! | NOTE: |
|---|---|
| Be wary of organizations that charge a fee to submit your application or to find you money for college. In general, the help you pay for can be obtained for free from your college or from Federal Student Aid. | If you or your family have unusual circumstances (such as loss of employment), complete *FAFSA on the Web* to the extent you can, then submit the application and consult the financial aid office at the college you plan to attend. |

### STATE AID DEADLINES

Check with your financial aid administrator for these states and territories:
AL, *AS, CO, *FM, GA, *GU, *HI, *MH, *MP, NC, NE, *NM, *NV, OR, PR, *PW, *SD, *TX, UT, *VA, *VI, *VT, WA, WI and *WY.

| | |
|---|---|
| AK | April 15, 2009 *(date received)* |
| AR | Academic Challenge - June 1, 2009 |
| | Workforce Grant - Contact your financial aid administrator |
| | Higher Education Opportunity Grant |
| | - June 1, 2009 (fall term) |
| | - November 1, 2009 (spring term) |
| | *(date received)* |
| AZ | March 1, 2009 *(date received)* |
| *CA | Initial awards - March 2, 2009 |
| | Additional community college awards |
| | - September 2, 2009 (date postmarked) |
| #*CT | February 15, 2009 *(date received)* |
| *DC | June 30, 2009 *(date received by state)* |
| DE | April 15, 2009 *(date received)* |
| FL | May 15, 2009 *(date processed)* |
| IA | July 1, 2009 *(date received)* |
| #*ID | Opportunity Grant - March 1, 2009 *(date received)* |
| #IL | First-time applicants - September 30, 2009 |
| | Continuing applicants - August 15, 2009 *(date received)* |
| IN | March 10, 2009 *(date received)* |
| #*KS | April 1, 2009 *(date received)* |
| #KY | March 15, 2009 *(date received)* |
| LA | July 1, 2009 *(date received)* |
| #MA | May 1, 2009 *(date received)* |
| MD | March 1, 2009 *(date received)* |
| ME | May 1, 2009 *(date received)* |
| MI | March 1, 2009 *(date received)* |
| MN | 30 days after term starts *(date received)* |
| MO | April 1, 2009 *(date received)* |
| #MS | MTAG and MESG Grants - September 15, 2009 |
| | HELP Scholarship - March 31, 2009 *(date processed)* |
| #MT | March 1, 2009 *(date received)* |
| ND | March 15, 2009 *(date received)* |
| NH | May 1, 2009 *(date received)* |
| NJ | June 1, 2009, if you received a Tuition Aid Grant in 2008 -2009 |
| | All other applicants |
| | - October 1, 2009, fall & spring terms |
| | - March 1, 2010, spring term only *(date received)* |
| *NY | May 1, 2010 *(date received)* |
| OH | October 1, 2009 *(date received)* |
| #OK | April 15, 2009 *(date received)* for best consideration |
| *PA | All 2008 - 2009 State Grant recipients & all non-2008 - 2009 State Grant recipients in degree programs - May 1, 2009 |
| | All other applicants - August 1, 2009 *(date received)* |
| #RI | March 1, 2009 *(date received)* |
| SC | Tuition Grants - June 30, 2009 *(date received)* |
| #TN | State Grant - March 1, 2009 |
| | State Lottery - September 1, 2009 *(date received)* |
| # *WV | March 1, 2009 *(date received)* |

# For priority consideration, submit application by date specified.

* Additional form may be required.

# Sample Free Application for Federal Student Aid (FAFSA)

## SECTION 1 – STUDENT INFORMATION

Questions are ordered as they appear on *FAFSA on the Web*, but after you are online you may be able to skip some questions based on your answers to earlier questions.

**Your last name** (Q1)

**Your Social Security Number** (Q8)

**Your driver's license number** (optional) (Q11)

**Are you a U.S. citizen?** (Q14)

If you are neither a citizen nor an eligible noncitizen, you are not eligible for federal student aid. However, you should still complete the application, because you may be eligible for state or college aid.

If you are in the U.S. on an F1 or F2 student visa, or a J1 or J2 exchange visitor visa, or a G series visa (pertaining to international organizations), you must answer "Neither citizen nor eligible noncitizen."

❏ U.S. citizen (U.S. national)

❏ Eligible noncitizen   Generally, you are an eligible noncitizen if you are:
- A permanent U.S. resident with a Permanent Resident Card (I-551);
- A conditional permanent resident (I-551C); or
- The holder of an Arrival-Departure Record (I-94) from the Department of Homeland Security showing any of the following designations: "Refugee," "Asylum Granted," "Parolee" (I-94 confirms paroled for a minimum of one year and status has not expired), "Victim of human trafficking," T-Visa holder (T-1, T-2, T-3, etc.) or "Cuban-Haitian Entrant."

❏ Neither citizen nor eligible noncitizen

**Your Alien Registration Number** (Q15)

If you are an eligible noncitizen, enter your eight- or nine-digit Alien Registration Number.

A

**What is your marital status as of today?** (Q16)

"As of today" refers to the day that you sign your FAFSA.

❏ Single, divorced or widowed
❏ Married or remarried   ❏ Separated

**Month and year you were married, separated, divorced or widowed** (Q17)

(Example: Month and year: 05/1998)

M M Y Y Y Y

**What is your state of legal residence?** (Q18)

**Enter the date you became a legal resident of your state if it was not before January 1, 2004.** (Q20) (Example: Month and year: 05/2005)

M M Y Y Y Y

Most male students must register with Selective Service to get federal aid. If you are male, age 18-25 and **NOT** registered, select "Register me." (Q22)

❏ Register me

**Have you ever received federal student aid?**

Answer "No" if you have never received federal student grants, federal student loans or federal work-study. You should also answer "No" if you have never attended college. If you answer "No" to this question, skip question 23.

❏ Yes
❏ No

**Have you been convicted for the possession or sale of illegal drugs for an offense that occurred while you were receiving federal student aid (grants, loans or work-study)?** (Q23)

Do not count convictions that have been removed from your record or that occurred before you turned age 18, unless you were tried as an adult. If you answer "Yes," you can use an interactive worksheet when completing the FAFSA online. Based on your answers to the worksheet questions, you can determine if the conviction affects your eligibility for federal student aid. If the conviction does affect your eligibility for federal aid, you should still submit your application because you may qualify for state or college aid.

❏ Yes

❏ No

**Highest school your father completed** (Q24)

Some states and colleges offer aid based on the level of schooling your parents completed.

❏ Middle school/Jr. high   ❏ College or beyond
❏ High school   ❏ Other/unknown

**Highest school your mother completed** (Q25)

Some states and colleges offer aid based on the level of schooling your parents completed.

❏ Middle school/Jr. high   ❏ College or beyond
❏ High school   ❏ Other/unknown

**When you begin the 2009-2010 school year, what degree or certificate will you be working on?** (Q29)

❏ 1st bachelor's degree
❏ 2nd bachelor's degree
❏ Associate degree (occupational or technical program)
❏ Associate degree (general education or transfer program)
❏ Certificate or diploma (occupational, technical or educational program of less than two years)

❏ Certificate or diploma (occupational, technical or educational program of two or more years)
❏ Teaching credential (nondegree program)
❏ Graduate or professional degree
❏ Other/undecided

## SECTION 1 (CONTINUED) – STUDENT INFORMATION

| | |
|---|---|
| **When you begin the 2009-2010 school year, what do you expect your enrollment status to be?** (Q30) <br> (Enrollment definitions refer to undergraduate study.) | ❑ Full-time (at least 12 credit hours in a term or 24 clock hours per week) <br> ❑ 3/4-time (at least 9 credit hours in a term or 18 clock hours per week) <br> ❑ Half-time (at least 6 credit hours in a term or 12 clock hours per week) <br> ❑ Less than half-time (fewer than 6 credit hours in a term or less than 12 clock hours per week) <br> ❑ Don't know |
| **In addition to grants, are you interested in being considered for work-study or student loans?** (Q31) | ❑ Work-study (aid earned through work)  ❑ Neither <br> ❑ Student loans (which you must pay back)  ❑ Don't know <br> ❑ Both work-study and student loans |

## SECTION 2 – STUDENT DEPENDENCY STATUS

| | |
|---|---|
| **Were you born before January 1, 1986?** (Q48) | ❑ Yes ❑ No |
| **As of today, are you married?** (Q49) <br><br> (Answer "Yes" if you are separated but not divorced.) "As of today" refers to the day that you sign your FAFSA. | ❑ Yes ❑ No |
| **At the beginning of the 2009-2010 school year, will you be working on a master's or doctorate program (such as an MA, MBA, MD, JD, PhD, EdD, graduate certificate, etc.)?** (Q50) | ❑ Yes ❑ No |
| **Are you currently serving on active duty in the U.S. Armed Forces for purposes other than training?** (Q51) | ❑ Yes ❑ No |
| **Are you a veteran of the U.S. Armed Forces?** (Q52) <br><br> Answer "Yes" (you are a veteran) if you (1) have engaged in active duty in the U.S. Armed Forces (Army, Navy, Air Force, Marines or Coast Guard) or are a National Guard or Reserve enlistee who was called to active duty for other than state or training purposes, or were a cadet or midshipman at one of the service academies, **and** (2) were released under a condition other than dishonorable. Also answer "Yes" if you are not a veteran now but will be by June 30, 2010. <br><br> Answer "No" (you are not a veteran) if you (1) have never engaged in active duty in the U.S. Armed Forces, (2) are currently an ROTC student or a cadet or midshipman at a service academy, (3) are a National Guard or Reserve enlistee activated only for state or training purposes, or (4) were engaged in active duty in the U.S. Armed Forces but released under dishonorable conditions. | ❑ Yes ❑ No |
| **Do you have children who will receive more than half of their support from you between July 1, 2009 and June 30, 2010?** (Q53) | ❑ Yes ❑ No |
| **Do you have dependents (other than your children or spouse) who live with you and who receive more than half of their support from you, now and through June 30, 2010?** (Q54) | ❑ Yes ❑ No |
| **At any time since you turned age 13, were both your parents deceased, were you in foster care or were you a dependent or ward of the court?** (Q55) <br><br> Answer "Yes" if you had no living parent (biological or adoptive) at any time since you turned age 13, even if you are now adopted. Answer "Yes" if you were in foster care at any time since you turned age 13, even if you are no longer in foster care as of today. Answer "Yes" if you were a dependent or ward of the court at any time since you turned age 13, even if you are no longer a dependent or ward of the court as of today. Note that the financial aid administrator at your school may require you to provide proof that you were in foster care or a dependent or ward of the court. | ❑ Yes ❑ No |
| **Use these instructions to answer questions 56-57** <br><br> Answer "Yes" if you can provide a copy of a court's decision that as of today you are an emancipated minor or are in legal guardianship. Also answer "Yes" if you can provide a copy of a court's decision that you were an emancipated minor or were in legal guardianship immediately before you reached the age of being an adult in your state. The court must be located in your state of legal residence at the time the court's decision was issued. | |
| **Are you or were you an emancipated minor as determined by a court in your state of legal residence?** (Q56) | ❑ Yes ❑ No |
| **Are you or were you in legal guardianship as determined by a court in your state of legal residence?** (Q57). | ❑ Yes ❑ No |
| **Use these instructions to answer questions 58-60** <br><br> Answer "Yes" if you received a determination at any time on or after July 1, 2008, that you were an unaccompanied youth who was homeless or, for question 60, at risk of being homeless. <br> • "Homeless" means lacking fixed, regular and adequate housing, which includes living in shelters, motels or cars, or temporarily living with other people because you had nowhere else to go. <br> • "Unaccompanied" means you are not living in the physical custody of your parent or guardian. <br> • "Youth" means you are 21 years of age or younger or you are still enrolled in high school as of the day you sign this application. | |
| **At any time on or after July 1, 2008, did your high school or school district homeless liaison determine that you were an unaccompanied youth who was homeless?** (Q58) | ❑ Yes ❑ No |
| **At any time on or after July 1, 2008, did the director of an emergency shelter or transitional housing program funded by the U.S. Department of Housing and Urban Development determine that you were an unaccompanied youth who was homeless?** (Q59) | ❑ Yes ❑ No |
| **At any time on or after July 1, 2008, did the director of a runaway or homeless youth basic center or transitional living program determine that you were an unaccompanied youth who was homeless or were self-supporting and at risk of being homeless?** (Q60) | ❑ Yes ❑ No |

If you answered "YES" to ANY of the previous questions, you do not have to provide parental information. Skip to Section 4 on page 6.
If you answered "NO" to ALL of the previous questions, then you must provide parental information. Complete Section 3 on the next page.

## SECTION 3 – PARENTAL INFORMATION

If you answered "No" to all of the questions in Section 2, you must provide parental information. Refer to your parents' IRS tax return when necessary. Answer the questions as of the date you will complete and sign your FAFSA.

- Grandparents, foster parents and legal guardians are not considered parents on this form unless they have legally adopted you.
- If your parent is widowed or single, answer the questions about that parent. If your widowed parent is remarried, answer the questions about that parent and your stepparent.
- If your parents are divorced or separated, answer the questions about the parent you lived with more during the past 12 months.    If you did not live with one parent more than the other, give answers about the parent who provided more financial support during the past 12 months. If this parent is remarried, answer the questions about that parent and your stepparent.

Federal law provides that, under very limited special circumstances, you may submit your FAFSA without parental information. If you have a special circumstance and are unable to provide parental information, *FAFSA on the Web* will instruct you on how to proceed. The following **are examples** of special circumstances.

- Your parents are incarcerated; or
- You have left home due to an abusive family environment; or
- You do not know where your parents are and are unable to contact them (and you have not been adopted).

| | |
|---|---|
| **What is your parents' marital status as of today?** (Q61)<br>"As of today" refers to the day that you sign your FAFSA. | ❏ Married or remarried  ❏ Divorced or separated<br>❏ Single  ❏ Widowed |
| **Month and year your parents were married, separated, divorced or widowed.**<br>(Q62) (Example: Month and year: 05/1998) | M M Y Y Y Y |
| **What is your parents' e-mail address?** (Q71)<br>If you provide your parents' e-mail address, we will let them know your FAFSA has been processed. | |
| **What is your father's (or stepfather's) Social Security Number?** (Q63) | ☐☐☐ - ☐☐ - ☐☐☐☐ |
| **What is your father's (or stepfather's) last name?** (Q64) | |
| **What is your father's (or stepfather's) date of birth?** (Q66)<br>(Example: Month, day and year: 05/07/1962) | M M D D Y Y Y Y |
| **What is your mother's (or stepmother's) Social Security Number?** (Q67) | ☐☐☐ - ☐☐ - ☐☐☐☐ |
| **What is your mother's (or stepmother's) last name?** (Q68) | |
| **What is your mother's (or stepmother's) date of birth?** (Q70)<br>(Example: Month, day and year: 05/07/1962) | M M D D Y Y Y Y |
| **What is your parents' state of legal residence?** (Q72) | |
| **Enter the date of legal residency for the parent who has lived in the state the longest, if it was not before January 1, 2004.** (Q74)<br>(Example: Month and year: 05/2005) | M M Y Y Y |

| **What income tax return did your parents file or will they file for 2008?** (Q83) | ❏ IRS 1040<br>❏ IRS 1040A, 1040EZ | ❏ A foreign tax return<br>❏ A tax return with Puerto Rico, another U.S. territory or a Freely Associated State |
|---|---|---|

| | |
|---|---|
| **If your parents have filed or will file a 1040, were they eligible to file a 1040A or 1040EZ?** (Q84)<br>A person is not eligible to file a 1040A or 1040EZ if he or she makes $100,000 or more, itemizes deductions, receives income from his or her own business or farm, is self-employed, receives alimony or is required to file Schedule D for capital gains. If your parents were not required to file a tax return or they filed a 1040 only to claim Hope or Lifetime Learning tax credits, and would have otherwise been eligible for a 1040A or 1040EZ, answer "Yes." | ❏ Yes<br>❏ No<br>❏ Don't know |
| **In 2007 or 2008, did you, your parents or anyone in your parents' household receive benefits from any of the federal benefits programs listed?** (Q77-81)<br>*Mark all the programs that apply.*<br>Select benefits received for all of your parents' household members. Include in your parents' household: (1) your parents and yourself, even if you don't live with your parents; (2) your parents' other children if (a) your parents will provide more than half of their support between July 1, 2009, and June 30, 2010, or (b) the children could answer "No" to every question in Section 2 of this worksheet; and (3) other people only if they live with your parents, your parents provide more than half of their support and your parents will continue to provide more than half of their support between July 1, 2009, and June 30, 2010. TANF may have a different name in your parents' state. Call 1-800-4-FED-AID to find out the name of the state's program. | ❏ Supplemental Security Income<br>❏ Food Stamps<br>❏ Free or Reduced Price School Lunch<br>❏ Temporary Assistance for Needy Families (TANF)<br>❏ Special Supplemental Nutrition Program for Women, Infants and Children (WIC) |

## SECTION 3 (CONTINUED) – PARENTAL INFORMATION

**As of today, is either of your parents a dislocated worker?** (Q85)

In general, a person may be considered a dislocated worker if he or she is receiving unemployment benefits due to being laid off or losing a job and is unlikely to return to a previous occupation; has been laid off or received a lay-off notice from a job; was self-employed but is now unemployed due to economic conditions or natural disaster; or is a displaced homemaker. A displaced homemaker is generally a person who previously provided unpaid services to the family (e.g., a stay-at-home mom or dad), is no longer supported by the husband or wife, is unemployed or underemployed and is having trouble finding or upgrading employment.

❑ Yes
❑ No
❑ Don't know

**What was your parents' adjusted gross income for 2008?** (Q86)

Adjusted gross income is on IRS form 1040—line 37; 1040A—line 21; or 1040EZ—line 4.

$ [        ]

**Questions 89 and 90** ask about earnings (wages, salaries, tips, etc.) in 2008.
Answer the questions whether or not a tax return was filed. This information may be on the W-2 forms, or on IRS Form 1040—lines 7 + 12 + 18 + Box 14 of IRS Schedule K-1 (Form 1065); 1040A—line 7; or 1040EZ—line 1.

**How much did your father/stepfather earn from working in 2008?** (Q89)

$ [        ]

**How much did your mother/stepmother earn from working in 2008?** (Q90)

$ [        ]

**Enter the amount of your parents' income tax for 2008.** (Q87)

Income tax amount is on IRS Form 1040—line 56; 1040A—line 35; or 1040EZ—line 11.

$ [        ]

**Enter your parents' exemptions for 2008.** (Q88)

Exemptions are on IRS Form 1040—line 6d or 1040A—line 6d. On the 1040EZ, if a person checked either the "you" or "spouse" box on line 5, use 1040EZ worksheet line F to determine the number of exemptions ($3,500 equals one exemption). If a person didn't check either box on line 5, enter 01 if he or she is single, or 02 if he or she is married.

[        ]

**Your parents' number of family members in 2009-2010.** (Q75)

Include in your parents' household: (1) your parents and yourself, even if you don't live with your parents, (2) your parents' other children if (a) your parents will provide more than half of their support between July 1, 2009, and June 30, 2010, or (b) the children could answer "No" to every question in Section 2 of this worksheet, and (3) other people only if they live with your parents, your parents provide more than half of their support and your parents will continue to provide more than half of their support between July 1, 2009, and June 30, 2010.

[        ]

**How many people in your parents' household will be college students between July 1, 2009 and June 30, 2010?** (Q76)

Always count yourself. **Do not include your parents.** Include others only if they will attend, at least half-time in 2009-2010, a program that leads to a college degree or certificate.

[        ]

**Your parents' 2008 Additional Financial Information (Q94)** Complete the left column of the table on page 8.

**Your parents' 2008 Untaxed Income (Q95)** Complete the left column of the table on page 8.

### Parent Asset Information

**As of today, what is your parents' total current balance of cash, savings and checking accounts?** (Q91)

$ [        ]

- Investments include real estate (do not include the family home), trust funds, UGMA and UTMA accounts, money market funds, mutual funds, certificates of deposit, stocks, stock options, bonds, other securities, Coverdell savings accounts, 529 college savings plans, the refund value of 529 prepaid tuition plans, installment and land sale contracts (including mortgages held), commodities, etc. For more information about reporting educational savings plans call 1-800-4-FED-AID. Investment value means the current balance or market value of these investments as of today. Investment debt means only those debts that are related to the investments.
- Do not include the value of life insurance, retirement plans (401[k] plans, pension funds, annuities, noneducation IRAs, Keogh plans, etc.) or cash, savings and checking accounts already reported in questions 41 and 91.
- Business and/or investment farm value includes the market value of land, buildings, machinery, equipment, inventory, etc. Business and/or investment farm debt means only those debts for which the business or investment farm was used as collateral.

**As of today, what is the net worth of your parents' investments, including real estate (not your parents' home)?** (Q92)

Net worth means current value minus debt.

$ [        ]

**As of today, what is the net worth of your parents' current businesses and/or investment farms?** (Q93)

**Do not include** the value of a family farm that your parents live on and operate.
**Do not include** the value of a small business if your family owns and controls more than 50 percent of the business and the business has 100 or fewer full-time or full-time equivalent employees. For small business value, your family includes (1) persons directly related to you, such as a parent, sister or cousin, or (2) persons who are or were related to you by marriage, such as a spouse, stepparent or sister-in-law.

$ [        ]

## SECTION 4 – STUDENT FINANCES

- Answer the questions as of the date you will complete and sign your FAFSA. Refer to the IRS tax return as needed.
- If you filed a foreign tax return, use the exchange rate at **www.federalreserve.gov/releases/h10/update** to convert monetary units to U.S. dollars.
- If you are married as of today, report your and your spouse's income, even if you were not married in 2008. Ignore references to spouse if you are single, divorced, separated or widowed.

| **What income tax return did you file or will you file for 2008?** (Q34) | ❏ IRS 1040<br>❏ IRS 1040A, 1040EZ<br>❏ A foreign tax return | ❏ A tax return with Puerto Rico, another U.S. territory or a Freely Associated State |
|---|---|---|

**If you have filed or will file a 1040, were you eligible to file a 1040A or 1040EZ?** (Q35)

A person is not eligible to file a 1040A or 1040EZ if he or she makes $100,000 or more, itemizes deductions, receives income from his or her own business or farm, is self-employed, receives alimony or is required to file Schedule D for capital gains. If you were not required to file a tax return or you filed a 1040 only to claim Hope or Lifetime Learning tax credits, and you would otherwise have been eligible for a 1040A or 1040EZ, answer "Yes."

❏ Yes
❏ No
❏ Don't know

**What was your (and your spouse's) adjusted gross income for 2008?** (Q36)

Adjusted gross income is on IRS Form 1040—line 37; 1040A—line 21; or 1040EZ—line 4.

$ 

**Questions 39 and 40** ask about earnings (wages, salaries, tips, etc.) in 2008. Answer the questions whether or not a tax return was filed. This information may be on the W-2 forms, or on IRS Form 1040—lines 7 + 12 + 18 + Box 14 of IRS Schedule K-1 (Form 1065); 1040A—line 7; or 1040EZ—line 1.

**How much did you earn from working in 2008?** (Q39)

$ 

**How much did your spouse earn from working in 2008?** (Q40)

$ 

**What type of veterans' education benefits will you receive?** (Q45)

Answer this question only if you will receive these benefits between July 1, 2009 and June 30, 2010.

❏ Montgomery GI Bill - Active Duty (Chapter 30)
❏ Post-9/11 GI Bill (Chapter 33)
❏ Montgomery GI Bill - Selected Reserve (Chapter 1606)
❏ Reserve Educational Assistance Program (Chapter 1607)
❏ Vocational Rehabilitation and Employment (Chapter 31)
❏ Dependents' Educational Assistance (Chapter 35)
❏ Any other type of veterans education benefits

**If you answered "YES" to ANY question in Section 2, answer the following questions.**
**If you answered "NO" to all the questions in Section 2, skip to page 7.**

**Your number of family members in 2009-2010.** (Q96)

Include in your household: (1) yourself (and your spouse), (2) your children, if you will provide more than half of their support between July 1, 2009, and June 30, 2010, and (3) other people if they now live with you, you provide more than half of their support and you will continue to provide more than half of their support between July 1, 2009, and June 30, 2010.

**How many people in your (and your spouse's) household will be college students between July 1, 2009 and June 30, 2010?** (Q97)

Always count yourself. Include others only if they will attend, at least half-time in 2009-2010, a program that leads to a college degree or certificate.

**In 2007 or 2008, did you (or your spouse) or anyone in your household (from question 96) receive benefits from any of the federal benefits programs listed?** (Q98-102) *Mark all the programs that apply.*

Select benefits received for all of your household members. Use the instructions in question 96 to identify who is included in your household. Answering these questions will not reduce your eligibility for student aid or these other federal benefits. TANF may have a different name in your state. Call 1-800-4-FED-AID to find out the name of your state's program.

❏ Supplemental Security Income
❏ Food Stamps
❏ Free or Reduced Price School Lunch
❏ Temporary Assistance for Needy Families (TANF)
❏ Special Supplemental Nutrition Program for Women, Infants and Children (WIC)

**As of today, are you (or your spouse) a dislocated worker?** (Q103)

In general, a person may be considered a dislocated worker if he or she is receiving unemployment benefits due to being laid off or losing a job and is unlikely to return to a previous occupation; has been laid off or received a lay-off notice from a job; was self-employed but is now unemployed due to economic conditions or natural disaster; or is a displaced homemaker. A displaced homemaker is generally a person who previously provided unpaid services to the family (e.g., a stay-at-home mom or dad), is no longer supported by the husband or wife, is unemployed or underemployed, and is having trouble finding or upgrading employment.

❏ Yes
❏ No
❏ Don't know

## SECTION 4 (CONTINUED) – STUDENT FINANCES

**Enter the amount of your (and your spouse's) income tax for 2008.** (Q37)
Income tax amount is on IRS Form 1040—line 56; 1040A—line 35; or 1040EZ—line 11.

$ _____

**Enter your (and your spouse's) exemptions for 2008.** (Q38)
Exemptions are on IRS Form 1040—line 6d or 1040A—line 6d. On the 1040EZ, if a person checked either the "you" or "spouse" box on line 5, use 1040EZ worksheet line F to determine the number of exemptions ($3,500 equals one exemption). If a person didn't check either box on line 5, enter 01 if he or she is single, or 02 if he or she is married.

_____

**Your 2008 Additional Financial Information amount (Q46)** Complete the right column of the table on page 8.

**Your 2008 Untaxed Income amount (Q47)** Complete the right column of the table on page 8.

### Student Asset Information (See "Parent Asset Information" on page 5 for instructions on reporting assets.)

**As of today, what is your (and your spouse's) total current balance of cash, savings and checking accounts?** (Q41) Do not include student financial aid.

$ _____

**As of today, what is the net worth of your (and your spouse's) investments, including real estate (not your home)?** (Q42) Net worth means current value minus debt.

$ _____

**As of today, what is the net worth of your (and your spouse's) current businesses and/or investment farms?** (Q43)

Do not include the value of a family farm that you (and your spouse) live on and operate.

Do not include the value of a small business if your family owns and controls more than 50 percent of the business and the business has 100 or fewer full-time or full-time equivalent employees. For small business value, your family includes (1) persons directly related to you, such as a parent, sister or cousin, or (2) persons who are or were related to you by marriage, such as a spouse, stepparent or sister-in-law.

$ _____

## SECTION 5 – COLLEGES TO RECEIVE INFORMATION

- If you do not know the school code, write the college's name. You will have a chance online to search for the school code.
- For each college, indicate the corresponding housing plan.

|  | 1st college | 2nd college | 3rd college | 4th college | 5th college |
|---|---|---|---|---|---|
| **Federal School Code** | _____ (Q104.a) | _____ (Q104.c) | _____ (Q104.e) | _____ (Q104.g) | _____ (Q104.i) |
| **Housing Plan** | ❑ on campus ❑ with parent ❑ off campus (Q104.b) | ❑ on campus ❑ with parent ❑ off campus (Q104.d) | ❑ on campus ❑ with parent ❑ off campus (Q104.f) | ❑ on campus ❑ with parent ❑ off campus (Q104.h) | ❑ on campus ❑ with parent ❑ off campus (Q104.j) |

|  | 6th college | 7th college | 8th college | 9th college | 10th college |
|---|---|---|---|---|---|
| **Federal School Code** | _____ (Q104.k) | _____ (Q104.m) | _____ (Q104.o) | _____ (Q104.q) | _____ (Q104.s) |
| **Housing Plan** | ❑ on campus ❑ with parent ❑ off campus (Q104.l) | ❑ on campus ❑ with parent ❑ off campus (Q104.n) | ❑ on campus ❑ with parent ❑ off campus (Q104.p) | ❑ on campus ❑ with parent ❑ off campus (Q104.r) | ❑ on campus ❑ with parent ❑ off campus (Q104.t) |

### Go to www.fafsa.ed.gov and enter the information from this worksheet.

Additional help is available online, or you can call 1-800-4-FED-AID. TTY users (hearing impaired) may call 1-800-730-8913. For more information on federal student aid, visit **www.FederalStudentAid.ed.gov**.

You can also talk with your college's financial aid office about other types of student aid that may be available.

## DO NOT MAIL THIS WORKSHEET.

# Sample Free Application for Federal Student Aid (FAFSA)

| | Use the tables below to report annual amounts. | |
|---|---|---|

For the Parents' column, enter the amount for the student's parent(s).  **For the Student's column, enter the amount for the student (and his or her spouse).**

| Parents' (Q94) | 2008 Additional Financial Information | Student's (Q46) |
|---|---|---|
| $ | a. Education credits (Hope and Lifetime Learning tax credits) from IRS Form 1040—line 50 or 1040A—line 31. | $ |
| $ | b. Child support paid because of divorce or separation or as a result of a legal requirement. <br> Don't include support for children in your (or your parents') household, as reported in question 96 (or question 75 for your parents). | $ |
| $ | c. Taxable earnings from need-based employment programs, such as Federal Work-Study and need-based employment portions of fellowships and assistantships. | $ |
| $ | d. Grant and scholarship aid reported to the IRS in the adjusted gross income. <br> Includes AmeriCorps benefits (awards, living allowances and interest accrual payments), as well as grant and scholarship portions of fellowships and assistantships. | $ |
| $ | e. Combat pay or special combat pay. <br> Only enter the amount that was taxable and included in the adjusted gross income. Do not enter untaxed combat pay reported on the W-2 (Box 12, Code Q). | $ |

| Parents' (Q95) | 2008 Untaxed Income | Student's (Q47) |
|---|---|---|
| $ | a. Payments to tax-deferred pension and savings plans (paid directly or withheld from earnings), including, but not limited to, amounts reported on the W-2 forms in Boxes 12a through 12d, codes D, E, F, G, H and S. | $ |
| $ | b. IRA deductions and payments to self-employed SEP, SIMPLE, Keogh and other qualified plans from IRS Form 1040—line 28 + line 32 or 1040A—line 17. | $ |
| $ | c. Child support received for all children. <br> Don't include foster care or adoption payments. | $ |
| $ | d. Tax exempt interest income from IRS Form 1040—line 8b or 1040A—line 8b. | $ |
| $ | e. Untaxed portions of IRA distributions from IRS Form 1040—lines (15a minus 15b) or 1040A—lines (11a minus 11b). <br> Exclude rollovers. If negative, enter a zero here. | $ |
| $ | f. Untaxed portions of pensions from IRS Form 1040—lines (16a minus 16b) or 1040A—lines (12a minus 12b). Exclude rollovers. If negative, enter a zero here. | $ |
| $ | g. Housing, food and other living allowances paid to members of the military, clergy and others (including cash payments and cash value of benefits). | $ |
| $ | h. Veterans noneducation benefits such as Disability, Death Pension, or Dependency & Indemnity Compensation (DIC) and/or VA Educational Work-Study allowances. | $ |
| $ | i. Other untaxed income not reported, such as workers' compensation, disability, etc. <br> **Don't include** student aid, earned income credit, additional child tax credit, welfare payments, untaxed Social Security benefits, Supplemental Security Income, Workforce Investment Act educational benefits, combat pay, benefits from flexible spending arrangements (e.g., cafeteria plans), foreign income exclusion or credit for federal tax on special fuels. | $ |
| XXXXXXXXXX | j. Money received, or paid on your behalf (e.g., bills), not reported elsewhere on this form. | $ |

# NOTES

# NOTES